MISNAMED
Misdiagnosed
Misunderstood

MISNAMED
Misdiagnosed
Misunderstood

**Recognizing and Coping with NVLD
(Nonverbal Learning Disorder)
from Childhood through Adulthood**

LINDA KARANZALIS, MS, BCCS
BOARD CERTIFIED COGNITIVE SPECIALIST WITH NVLD

Heerlen
Publishing

Misnamed, Misdiagnosed, Misunderstood:
Recognizing and Coping with NVLD (Nonverbal Learning Disorder)
from Childhood through Adulthood

Copyright © 2022 by Linda Karanzalis

All rights reserved

No portion of this book may be reproduced, stored in
a retrieval system, or transmitted in any form by any
means–electronic, mechanical, photocopy, recording,
or other–except for brief quotations in printed reviews,
without prior permission of the author.

First Edition

Hardcover ISBN: 979-8-9868018-1-0
Paperback ISBN: 979-8-9868018-0-3
eBook ISBN: 979-8-9868018-2-7

The information provided in this book is for informational purposes only and is not intended to diagnose, treat, cure, or be a replacement for legal or medical advice. The author specifically disclaims any liability, directly or indirectly, for the use and application of any of the contents of this book.

To my dad and my hero, Bernard Ronciglione
"Keep It Simple"
"You Had to Be There"
September 27, 1921–February 20, 2021

To my mother, Pieta Ronciglione,
for her bravery working with her family
and the Dutch Resistance
to save lives during the Holocaust
February 6, 1928–February 1, 2022

Acknowledgments

I am grateful to the following people:

- Sari Solden for being a role model to me and for her encouragement and groundbreaking work for the benefit of neurodiverse women with ADHD

- Diane Alessi for her contributions, professional feedback, and guidance, and for being an advocate of my work

- Kate Conn for her heartfelt contributions and feedback

- Linda Fallo-Mitchell for her commitment to this book

- The NVLD Project for advocating to get the NVLD diagnosis in the DSM

In recognition of the NVLD Pioneers,
you are forging new territory for
not only yourselves but those who follow you.

For my clients and students,
It has been an honor to serve you.
Thank you for all you have taught me.
Your courage and success are my rewards.

Special shout-outs to:
- Anna, for providing me valuable resources
- Anne-Marie, for coming into my life with her giving heart
- Anthony, for looking out for me during my vulnerable teenage years
- Anthony Williams, for giving me back my health and my ability to help others
- Becky, for her guidance over the years
- Beth, for her encouragement to keep on going
- Betsy, for her support and stroller treats
- Kathy, for helping me to brainstorm color schemes and layouts
- Celeste, for helping my mother to take care of me as child and for validating me during my formative years
- Donna, my biggest fan and cheerleader
- Jamie, Melissa, and Stu for keeping up my morale
- Juliet, for letting me be the "director" and her unwavering support over the years
- Karen, for her kindness and assistance
- Kim, for her enthusiastic and experiential input

- Matthew, for his unconditional love and bringing out the best in everyone
- Nick, for coming into my life and helping me behind the scenes with his skills to impact others
- Rich, for his confidence and support as I struggled to finish this book
- Rob, for his endless faith in my ability to succeed
- Sharon, for her encouragement and keeping me on track
- Stephanie, for her inspirational input
- Theresa, for willingness to learn about NVLD
- Yia Yia, for her consistent support during my college years
- To all those, as there are too many to mention, who have supported me on my journey
- Last, but not least, for the cowgirl who lassoed me in at the last-minute and saved the day

Professional Praise

Vivid, compelling, poignant, full of heart and fresh understanding. But also full of current science and all the evidence any novitiate might need. It's the first book that explained NVLD to me in a way that I could actually understand and get excited about. I now understand it so well that I concluded I have the condition myself! Karanzalis is fervent in her desire to replace suffering, misunderstanding, and frustration with triumph, clarity, and sweet success for the millions of people who have NVLD as well as those who care about them. Bravo, Linda Karanzalis! In my book, you are a valiant crusader and an educator of heroic proportions.

**—Edward Hallowell, MD,
child and adult psychiatrist,
world-renowned expert on ADHD,
and author of the *New York Times* bestseller
Driven to Distraction and *ADHD 2.0***

Misnamed, Misdiagnosed, Misunderstood: Recognizing and Coping with NVLD (Nonverbal Learning Disorder) from Childhood through Adulthood is a must read for individuals with NVLD, parents and family members of children with NVLD, and their teachers/co-workers.

Linda explains NVLD to both neuro-typical (NT) and neuro-divergent (ND) individuals in a personal, thoughtful, and understandable way. She takes the reader (both NT and

ND) through the thought process of confronting and coming to terms with the fact that they have NVLD, seamlessly weaving solid research into her many stories. Through concrete, down-to-earth, and sometimes humorous examples, Linda presents information with which people can identify; I especially enjoyed the sections dealing with social struggles and how to overcome them.

This is a complete seminar on NVLD in a book! It walks parents through the expected developmental and educational stages of NVLD, providing checklists to help people determine if and when further neuropsychological evaluation is needed. It will help you to become a better advocate for your child and will instruct you in how to protect your child from the perils that lie ahead.

Having worked with children and adults with NVLD for more than 40 years, I know that this book provides a compassionate view into their challenges while providing everyday doable 'work arounds' and I will be personally recommending it to those with whom I work.

—Dean J. M. Mooney, Ph.D., NCSP,
Licensed Clinical Psychologist,
Nationally Certified School Psychologist, and
coauthor of *Nonverbal Learning Disabilities;*
A Guide to School Success

This unique book will help people with NVLD, their parents, teachers, and their loved ones understand this complex disorder. Karanzalis uses her personal experiences across the developmental stages of childhood to college to early adulthood to lay out practical solutions for people who have NVLD (soon to be renamed DVSP). Her work as a professional with formal education, extensive research, and clinical practice make her uniquely qualified to provide assistance for those with similar experiences. She warmly offers to be your guide, providing information that will help you understand yourself and help others understand you. She knows that being misunderstood causes suffering, but understanding leads to peace of mind. Linda uses her own personal experience as well as numerous case examples from her practice to identify and clarify the best strategies for success. It is a great addition and contribution to the field.

—Dr. Jessica Broitman, researcher, clinician, coauthor of *NVLD and Developmental Visual-Spatial Disorder in Children: Clinical Guide to Assessment and Treatment,* **and a member of the Columbia University consortium working for the inclusion of NVLD in the DSM**

The new book, *Misnamed, Misdiagnosed, Misunderstood: Recognizing and Coping with NVLD (Nonverbal Learning Disorder) from Childhood through Adulthood* by Linda Karanzalis, is as inspirational as it is informative, and I highly recommend it for adults with NVLD, parents, and professionals. Ms. Karanzalis is obviously an expert on the subject, but more than that, she is a role model who guides readers through this very difficult terrain while managing, by her own example, to instill hope, insight, and courage.

Often misunderstood, missed completely, or confused with other closely related challenges, NVLD can cause emotional distress, impact careers, damage relationships, and diminish one's sense of self. This book supplies much-needed clarity to aid in both diagnosis and guidance. The author's practical strategies are steeped in deep understanding so they never feel superficial. Most importantly, Ms. Karanzalis, by her brave and open disclosures and poignant stories of her own journey as well as those of the countless others she has helped, provides an encouraging voice that inspires the readers to forge their own unique path.

—Sari Solden, MS, psychotherapist, consultant, speaker, author of *Women with ADHD: Journeys through ADDulthood*, and the coauthor of *A Radical Guide for Women with ADHD*

This is a timely and terrific book. Linda Karanzalis is a board certified cognitive specialist and expert on NVLD and a leader in support of both children and adults with nonverbal learning disorder. As she points out, this diagnosis has been around for years, yet has not been included in diagnostic manuals. This leaves families floundering when their child's needs are poorly understood and supported. With this book, Linda fills that gap.

Linda writes from the heart. She has lived with the challenges of nonverbal learning disorder all of her life. After defining NVLD and listing the key features, Linda recounts experiences from her own life as a child, teenager, and adult with NVLD and ADHD. Incorporating the experiences of others who have shared her struggles and found effective strategies of their own reminds the reader that every person with NVLD is uniquely themselves, and there are many ways to find success. These stories will resonate for many parents, and the strategies given are golden.

—Robin E. McEvoy, Ph.D,
developmental neuropsychologist, and
coauthor of *Child Decoded; Unlocking Complex Issues*
in Your Child's Learning, Behavior, or Attention

Linda Karanzalis is an ideal guide to the often neglected and poorly understood world of what is currently termed Non-Verbal Learning Disability (NVLD). Writing from her own personal experience, as well as with the expertise of a professional educator, she offers understanding, insight, and hope for those with this diagnosis and their families.

—Jeremy Veenstra-VanderWeele, M.D.,
Child, Adolescent, and Adult Psychiatrist;
Director of the Division of Child &
Adolescent Psychiatry, Columbia University

It's rare to find an education expert whose expertise is rooted in her own experience of NVLD, a brain-based communication and learning issue. One of the few nationally recognized experts on this misunderstood diagnosis, Linda Karanzalis pioneered innovative interventions for NVLD that have helped countless of children, teens, and adults live more successful, happier, and fulfilled lives.

**—Tracy Otsuka, JD, LLM, AACC,
host of the *ADHD for Smart Ass Women* podcast,
globally ranked in the top 0.5 percent of
all podcasts in the world on any subject**

What Her Clients Say about Linda Karanzalis, MS, BCCS

We were so blessed to have met Linda when our son was young. Jeffrey was diagnosed with ADD when he was eight years old and, later, with NVLD. Linda helped us to understand that his brain worked differently. She gave us the tools so we could learn how to deal with things from his perspective. Our son would never listen to us, but he listened to Linda because he knew she really understood. Through coaching with Linda, we learned how to work with our son during some very difficult times, and she never made us feel like we were bad parents.

—Jane Plunkitt

When our daughter, Sydney, was sixteen years old, she was struggling socially and emotionally and could not find the motivation that she once had. When we received the results of her assessment, there was strong evidence to suggest NVLD. The therapists we consulted were not familiar with the diagnosis and were uncertain of the correct treatment plan. We were at a loss as to how to help Sydney until we found Linda.

—Marie West

Linda has been a blessing to my family, guiding us through our difficult NVLD journey with her expertise and experience. She is understanding and extremely passionate about NLVD and the struggles it brings. She set us on a path that cultivated success through thinking outside the box. Linda gave us the knowledge and resources we never knew existed, which helped our son academically and socially. Forever grateful.

—Kathy Mills

Our twenty-five-year-old son was having trouble getting his life together. He has ADHD, NVLD, and anxiety. We never knew he had NVLD until we met Linda. She worked with him for a couple of years, meeting with him, doing various programs, coaching him, and giving behavioral feedback to his doctor. As a result, our son has made some real progress, becoming more social and organized. He even started doing stand-up comedy! I'm definitely grateful for Linda's help.

—Rachel Mercanti

Linda helped us in many different ways. She explained that dealing with NVLD and ADHD requires many different tactics. There is no single magical thing that can help your neurodivergent child, but there are several things that can help. I learned how important diet and supplements are and how to use essential oils for my child. Linda coached me on how to help and guide my child all the while offering support whenever it was needed. I am grateful to have been referred to Linda. I know that my child and I have benefited greatly from Linda's expertise and support. I also know that if I call her, she will never run out of ideas.

—Dara Robinson

I have anxiety, NVLD, and ADHD. Linda coached me by monitoring my progress through her program and instructing me remotely online. She was readily available for me whenever I needed her. I get anxious and overwhelmed quickly, and Linda has helped me rationalize and put my thoughts together in a more organized way. Since I began working with Linda, I have been able to hold down a job and attend college full-time. I feel more confident because I have begun to improve my abilities since I began to accomplish my goals, which has greatly lessened my anxieties about the future. I'm so grateful to be receiving her guidance.

—Jacob Kavky

We have been working with Linda for a few months now. I say "we" because Linda has become an invaluable resource for both my teenagers with ADHD, NVLD, and executive functioning challenges and for me, a mom supporting them. Linda is full of incredibly helpful resources that have improved my son's brain functions, accountability, and productivity at home and school. Her upbeat personality and flexible nature make her a pleasure to work with. We are in it for the long haul, and I can't imagine working with anyone else.

—Donna Harper

There is not enough room on this paper to list all of the changes and improvements that have occurred since my son began to work with Linda Karanzalis. He has shown improvements across the board and is more confident, independent, and focused.

—Tom Badges

Since my child started to work with Linda, it is easier to get him to do things, which was a struggle in the past. He is less depressed, and I hear him laughing more. I interpret this as a decrease in his frustration level because tasks have generally become easier for him.

—Regina Lyons

As soon as our son started to work with Linda, his enthusiasm improved, his memory sharpened, he was able to persevere at tasks, and his ability to reason and understand logic increased. He realized he was intelligent and understood that he simply needed some assistance to unlock his brain. I just loved working with Linda and have recommended her to others. She has taught me a lot, and our son is doing great!

—Amy Ritts

Jessica's biggest improvements were in math. She can now work through difficult problems and is capable of doing her homework independently and twice as fast. All of her teachers have reported better classroom performance and increased sociability.

—Susan Byers

Before Katie began working with Linda, she was having difficulty completing assignments and staying focused on tasks. We began to see improvements in the third week. After the fourth week, the teacher called us to let us know that she had made significant improvements. Katie made the honor roll on her last marking period in the fourth grade. She also has better comprehension than ever before and has become more social as well.

—Megan McCann

I really appreciate everything Linda did for me. Attending graduate school with a learning disability and ADHD was difficult, but she was very accommodating of my schedule and helped me to continue to improve my processing speed and executive functioning skills. My family also noticed a difference in my improved abilities! Overall, I am very grateful for her help.

—John Anderson

"Autobiography in Five Short Chapters" by Portia Nelson[1]

I came across this poem years ago; it spoke to me about the pain I was feeling. It's not specifically about NVLD, but it comforted me to know I wasn't alone. When you read "it is my fault," don't take it to mean that you caused your setbacks. The message for me was and still is that even though NVLD wasn't my fault, I am responsible for managing my responses to the problems NVLD caused me. I hope this poem provides you with the same comfort and inspiration as it did for me.

> **Autobiography in Five Chapters**
> Chapter I
> I walk down the street.
> There is a deep hole in the sidewalk.
> I fall in.
> I am lost…I am hopeless.
> It isn't my fault.
> It takes forever to find a way out.
> Chapter II
> I walk down the same street.

---

[1] Portia Nelson, "Autobiography in Five Chapters," *There's a Hole in My Sidewalk: The Romance of Self-Discovery* (Middlebury Press, 2010).

There is a deep hole in the sidewalk.
I pretend I don't see it.
I fall in again.
I can't believe I am in the same place.
But, it isn't my fault.
It still takes me a long time to get out.

Chapter III

I walk down the same street
There is a deep hole in the sidewalk.
I see it is there.
I still fall in. It's a habit.
My eyes are open.
I know where I am.
It is my fault. I get out immediately.

Chapter IV

I walk down the same street.
There is a deep hole in the sidewalk.
I walk around it.

Chapter V

I walk down another street.

Contents

Author's Note xxvii
Why I Wrote This Book 1
Chapter 1:   Don't Judge a Book by Its Cover 7
Chapter 2:   Is It You, Me, or NVLD? 37
Chapter 3:   The Home Front 51
Chapter 4:   School Daze: Why Can't I Be Like
             Everyone Else? 63
Chapter 5:   Finding the Right Job 95
Chapter 6:   Friendships and Relationships 125
Chapter 7:   Masking and the Struggle for
             Emotional Well-Being 147
Chapter 8:   Humpty Dumpty: Putting Yourself
             Together Again 169
Chapter 9:   Mind, Body, Spirit: Healing Your
             Whole Self 199
Chapter 10: Telling It Like It Is: Everyday NVLD 221
Resources for Support and Information 243
Author's Note 247

Author's Note

If you're anything like me and skim through a book trying to capture the take-home points, please don't. Every page is a must-read! So grab a cup of coffee and get yourself comfortable in order to better understand this little-known "thing" called nonverbal learning disorder (NVLD).

Why I Wrote This Book

Once upon a time, a little girl named Linda was afraid to go to school. She struggled to pay attention, make sense of what she needed to learn, and understand how to interact with other children. She was bullied and developed an ulcer. But because she was a well-behaved child who worked hard in school, adults did not see or address her educational and social challenges, and she "slipped through the cracks."

That little girl was me!

In my early thirties, I was diagnosed with nonverbal learning disorder (NVLD), a brain-based learning disorder. It was only then that I understood I wasn't imagining things or thinking too much—I was trying to survive. Despite my above-average intelligence, I thought I was intellectually impaired. From childhood through my twenties, I lived in despair; now as an education professional in the field of neurodiversity, I live up to my potential.

My passion and life's mission are to help others; that's why I became a public-school special education teacher, a master's level brain-based educator, and a board certified cognitive specialist. I have worked with hundreds of parents, students, and adults to improve the quality of their lives academically, socially, emotionally, and financially. It is my hope that, through the story of my journey and those of my clients, this book will bring attention to NVLD and empower others to improve their lives or the lives of their children, students, or clients. With an accurate diagnosis and treatment intervention, these individuals can be spared years of frustration and downward spirals and go on to lead meaningful, fulfilling, and productive lives.

This book goes to press just as NVLD has become part of the national conversation. At the televised 2022 Academy Awards, Will Smith attacked Chris Rock over a joke about Smith's wife. Weeks later, Rock says he is still processing what happened.

Rock had publicly shared his NVLD diagnosis in 2020, but the attention NVLD received at that time pales in comparison to the global clamor for information and clarity about the disorder following "the slap" that was heard around the world. Since then, internet searches for NVLD have risen sharply, and people have shared information about NVLD on social media. Rock's Twitter page now features a link to the NVLD Project's (national nonprofit) website.

This is a book that confirms it's not all in your head. There is a reason for the social and academic difficulties experienced by individuals with average to superior verbal intelligence. There is an explanation for personal struggles with organization, executive functioning, nonverbal communication, visual-spatial skills, and social situations that accompany high-level verbal language skills: NVLD.

> Currently NVLD is *not* included in either the World Health Organization's *International Classification of Diseases* or the American Psychiatric Association's *Diagnostic and Statistical Manual of Mental Disorders (DSM)*, thus hindering the provision of a diagnosis and services for individuals with these traits.

NVLD, attention deficit hyperactivity disorder (ADHD), and autism share some of the same symptoms. However, there are significant differences in brain biology among the three disorders. NVLD encompasses a broad range of challenges and behaviors, so you may not relate to all of the examples in this book. No two people, even those with NVLD, are alike.

Much of the information I'm sharing comes from my experiences growing up with a nonverbal learning disorder and the journey I took to where I am today. I was stumbling along in life, unable to figure out why things others could do easily were so incredibly difficult and painful for me. Like a pioneer, I had to forge a new path to understand and master my NVLD. Perseverance and hard work led me to the answers I needed. Through this process, I found the validation I needed to move forward. Knowing that "it's not your fault, and you didn't do anything wrong" is tremendously empowering. As a professional, I now help those with NVLD and other brain-based disorders to minimize their struggles and maximize their successes.

Many NVLDers out there are the "walking wounded." Parents are desperate to help their children, both young and adult, who have slipped through the cracks and are experiencing pain and rejection, despite their best efforts. These parents also often suffer from stress, depression, anxiety, and other mental health challenges when they are unable to help their kids. Many of these children will continue to live at home, struggling well into adulthood, and will need ongoing support.

Adult NVLDers who are working through challenges on their own, with or without support from their parents or professionals, watch as their peers pass them by. Their classmates, team members, and neighbors progress from grade school to high school, from college to careers, from living with their parents to living on their own, from dating to marriage to parenting, from making acquaintances to building lasting friendships, from professional advancement to financial gains, and from renting to owning their homes. It is my intention that this book provides much of the support they should have had and didn't.

Is it any wonder these souls wind up with mental illness, including depression, anxiety, PTSD, learned helplessness, codependency, and other conditions?

If you are not diagnosed with NVLD but suspect that you may have it, this book will help you obtain the correct diagnosis. What is important is that you start wherever you are and recognize that, with the right support, and an open mind, you can navigate the challenges. It has been estimated that people with NVLD are unable to process a significant amount (some researchers say as high as 93 percent) of nonverbal communication. Nonverbal communication (body language, tone of voice, gestures) changes the meaning of spoken words, causing those with NVLD to continually misunderstand others. Self-acknowledgment and education about NVLD go hand in hand with other tools to move forward.

Many of the principles I'm sharing with you will not be found elsewhere. This is not a book about scientific research; it's a practical approach to understanding NVLD, its issues, and the internal struggles. Just like Rocky Balboa trained, fought, ran, and boxed his way to his first championship, you'll learn what works and doesn't work based on the unique challenges you face as an individual. Applying the concepts outlined in this book can save you years of frustration and backpedaling.

In this book, you will also find specific tools that go beyond using strategies. While strategies are necessary, they typically are not enough to help you reach your potential. You are going to find real-life examples of people of all ages who have been affected by NVLD. The names have been changed, and each represents a composite profile of those with NVLD and co-occurring conditions I have encountered since 1991. Their experiences might give you the comfort, as a parent of a child with NVLD or an adult with NVLD, that you are not alone and the inspiration to take steps toward your goals.

When I was young, I went to hell and back by virtue of the many difficulties I faced. My personal experiences from childhood to college to early adulthood and my endeavors as a professional with formal education, extensive research experience, and clinical practice make me uniquely qualified to provide assistance for those with similar experiences.

Think about being in a foreign country where you don't speak the native language. You may need to use a translation app or ask a local to show you around. Or you might choose tours so you can relax while you learn about your surroundings. I will be your guide, offering information that will help you understand yourself and help others understand you. Being misunderstood causes suffering; understanding leads to peace of mind and clarity. Start the next phase of your journey with me.

NVLD is interchangeably referred to as nonverbal learning disorder and nonverbal learning disability. In this book, NVLD will be referred to as nonverbal learning disorder.

Chapter 1

Don't Judge a Book by Its Cover

We've all heard the saying "Don't judge a book by its cover," but that's exactly what happens in our society. Within seconds of meeting someone, our minds automatically form our first impression of that person.

As a result of our tendency to judge a book by its cover, people with NVLD are often misunderstood. Most people have experienced the embarrassment of misreading social cues, but for those with NVLD, this can be an ongoing and chronic problem, and they may be misperceived as difficult, rude, bossy, incompetent, clueless, lazy, or crazy. Changing others' perceptions is much harder for those with NVLD, because their behavior does not match any visible sign of deficits, thereby denying them the understanding they need for a good first impression. Those misperceptions result in missed opportunities and lost relationships.

Opening the Book

People who think, learn, and do things differently from the majority of the population (neurotypicals, or NTs) because of neurological differences are known as neurodivergent (ND). Those with NVLD are therefore categorized as ND. Since their appearance doesn't indicate the discrepancy between their exceptional verbal communication and their poor nonverbal communication (body language, facial expressions, gestures, tone of voice) and performance difficulties, people assume they are neurotypical.

NVLD may be the most overlooked, misunderstood, misdiagnosed, and misnamed learning disability. According to "Estimated Prevalence of Nonverbal Learning Disability among North American Children and Adolescents," published in the April 2020 issue of the *Journal of the American Medical Association* (*JAMA*), between 2.2 and 2.9 million children under the age of eighteen in the United States and Canada may have NVLD. Moreover, as many as 50 percent of them have received no diagnosis. Overlapping symptoms and co-occurring disorders may cause those with NVLD to be misdiagnosed as having ADHD or autism level 1 (a variant of autism formerly known as Asperger's syndrome) and therefore, NVLD to be underdiagnosed. Marcia Rubinstein, an education specialist in West Hartford, Connecticut, once said that almost every child she saw with NVLD had first been diagnosed with ADHD.

Despite the overlapping symptoms in all of these disorders, the causes stem from differences in brain pathology that distinguish one disorder from another. A nonverbal learning disability is believed to be caused by damage, disorder, or destruction of neuronal white matter in the brain's right hemisphere. In an article published in the March 1, 1994, *Journal of Learning Disabilities*, Michael C. S. Harnadek and Bryan P. Rourke wrote that brain scans have identified that children with NVLD have smaller splenia than those with high-functioning autism and ADHD. The splenium is a part of the corpus callosum that connects the left and right hemispheres of the brain and is vital for visual-spatial functioning. NVLD typically shows up as a right-hemisphere weakness.

Adding to the confusion is disagreement among professionals within the psychological and educational communities. Since NVLD is not included in the *Diagnostic and Statistical Manual of Mental Disorders* (*DSM*), it isn't recognized as an official disorder. The *DSM* is the bible of mental disorders, used by professionals as a reference for descriptions, symptoms, and criteria to make an official diagnosis required for insurance reimbursement and approval of special education services. But not all children and adults fit into the same pattern. In other words, NVLD is not a cookie-cutter diagnosis. The saying "When you've met one person with autism, you've met one person" also applies to those with NVLD.

NVLD is distinguished by both visual-spatial and nonverbal communication skills deficits, according to experts at the National Center for Learning Disabilities. The NVLD Project's website states that one defining criterion for the condition is the presence of a discrepancy between perceptual reasoning (formerly performance IQ) and verbal comprehension (formerly verbal IQ), as measured by intelligence tests. The VIQ-PIQ discrepancy is the single agreed-upon feature necessary for a diagnosis of NVLD.

Ray

Research has shown that, in this society, attractive people are well received and afforded more opportunities. This was the case with Ray, one of my students with NVLD. He was a beautiful child with perfectly chiseled features. He was so good-looking his mother was often told he could be a model. On first meeting Ray, most people assumed that he was well-behaved and neurotypical, making that assessment solely based on his appearance. People did not expect him to behave as he did. In fact, due to his appearance, they expected more of him and were often confused by the discrepancy between his appearance and his behaviors. Because Ray is neurodivergent (ND), his literal interpretations, hyperactivity, impulsivity, and lack of focus caused him, at times, to unintentionally blurt out blunt and tactless comments.

When we see someone in a wheelchair, we don't hold that person accountable for things they struggle with or cannot do. Most of us understand they may need assistance and alter our expectations accordingly. Wouldn't it be crazy and cruel to blame and reject a person for being unable to walk, as if she is doing it on purpose? Yet Ray was identified as a "spoiled brat" and his mother as a bad parent.

There is no such sign or visible evidence, like a wheelchair, to account for NVLDers' difficulties and socially awkward behaviors. The depression, learned helplessness, broken friendships, countless jobs, rejections, crippling anxiety, and ongoing therapy with little to no results would wear down anyone. They begin to doubt and blame themselves and may question their sanity, wondering why they are underestimated and misconstrued.

A Work in Progress

The NVLD Project, a nonprofit organization, is working hard to bring about positive change and acceptance in society for those with NVLD. They've funded researchers from Columbia University to conduct the scientific research needed to secure inclusion of NVLD in the *DSM* (*Diagnostic and Statistical Manual of Mental Disorders*).

As of this writing, a proposal has been submitted to the *DSM* Steering Committee of the American Psychiatric Association to include NVLD, renamed as developmental visual-spatial disorder (DVSD), in future versions of the *DSM* diagnostic system. The consensus diagnostic criteria set for DVSD was formulated with input from experts in NVLD, learning disabilities, and neurodevelopmental disorders.

I'm proud to be an ambassador for the NVLD Project, helping to spread awareness by advocating for inclusion, understanding, and treatment so that NVLDers can become productive members of society and live their best lives. *(cont'd)*

> Visit the NVLD Project's website (https://nvld.org/) to learn more about the disorder and donate in support of their efforts in research, education, and community outreach. You can also donate to them on my website at https://www.lindakaranzalis.com on the footer of my page.

Yes, We Speak!

The current name of this neurodevelopmental disorder is a misleading term, as it implies people with NVLD don't speak. Parents, teachers, and therapists are often dumbfounded when I'm talking about myself as someone who has NVLD. "What do you mean? You can talk!" they say. That may be one reason why some want to change NVLD to developmental visual-spatial disorder.

NVLDers have exceptional vocabularies, expressive language, and auditory memory. In fact, most have an impressive range of knowledge in many different areas. It is often virtually inconceivable to others that these individuals have significant difficulties functioning day to day. Although having average to superior verbal intelligence, NVLDers have difficulties with visual-spatial processing, executive functioning (planning and prioritizing), recognizing and processing nonverbal social communication cues (facial expressions, body language, tone of voice), academics, motor skills, social-emotional learning, higher-order thinking (forming conclusions from facts), and mathematical concepts.

Because of their significant difficulty processing nonverbal communication, which often changes the speaker's spoken message, they frequently make inaccurate conclusions when communicating with others. This in turn impacts their ability to effectively respond and express emotions, opinions, intentions, and ideas within the context of a conversation.

Danielle

Danielle cannot decipher others' nonverbal communication without asking clarifying questions. Danielle doesn't know it, but her coworkers call her "Ditsy Danielle" behind her back. They think she just doesn't listen. People often feel she is challenging them and accuse her of being difficult.

Her poor visual-spatial skills often cause her to invade the personal space boundaries of others, which makes them uncomfortable. Danielle is unable to operate the office copying machine successfully because she cannot decipher the pictorial troubleshooting icons to fix paper jams and other malfunctions. To avoid embarrassment by continually asking for help, she leaves the machine as is and waits until someone else fixes it. Her coworkers think she is lazy.

The 7-38-55 Percent Rule

Albert Mehrabian, Ph.D, a professor emeritus at UCLA, published a book in 1971 called *Silent Messages: Implicit Communication of Emotions and Attitudes*. In the book, he stated that most people process and understand communication in three ways: verbal (7 percent), nonverbal (55 percent), and tone of voice and rate of speech (38 percent). That breakdown became the gold standard for understanding human communication, partly because it is an easy formula to remember.

Though his studies are quoted as expert opinion, Dr. Mehrabian's conclusions never made sense to me. In other words, if it is true that 93 percent of communication is nonverbal, you should be able to understand the meaning of a movie or a play simply by observing the body language of the actors without hearing the dialogue.

Dr. Mehrabian said these statistics do not mean that body language and vocal variety is more important than spoken words. These percentages apply only to emotions and attitudes in the relationship between spoken words and facial expressions and between two people when determining whether they like or dislike one another. I see this difficulty in my work. Many of my clients struggle to identify how the person they are speaking to feels about them and what they are saying. Being unable to discern this puts them in the unfortunate position of not knowing how to respond to others in a myriad of situations and relationships.

In my opinion, the research on how much communication is verbal versus how much is nonverbal needs to be redone. Dr. Mehrabian's work was misunderstood and misapplied and is still being incorrectly used by some professionals—and not just those in the NVLD community. This isn't to blame anyone, as there are so many sources that refer to this research as the truth that the myth continues.

In 2014, Scott Rouse, a behavior analyst and body language expert who has trained professionals in the FBI, Secret Service, US Military Intelligence, and the Department of Defense, presented a TEDx Talk called "How to Kill Your Body Language Frankenstein (and Inspire the Villagers)." Rouse believes that misinterpreted body language causes problems with friends, family, and coworkers, and that's why we can't apply the misinterpreted research of Dr. Mehrabian.

In the talk, Rouse illuminates why the standard methods of interpreting body language can be misleading. For example, most NTs assume that when the other person crosses their arms across their chest, they are not open to hearing what is being said to them, when in fact they may be fascinated by the conversation, or they may just be cold. The confusion doesn't stop there for NVLDers, who may also be unable to ascertain the other person's motive.

Despite the overlap of shared symptoms, autism and NVLD are not the same. NVLDers have impaired visual-spatial processing, while those on the spectrum typically have strengths in this area. Therefore, having the correct diagnosis is imperative to receive appropriate intervention services. Understandably, many with NVLD are diagnosed as autistic to obtain educational and support services, but a diagnosis of autism is insufficient to meet all of the needs of those with NVLD.

Moreover, it may not apply at all: One research study, "Epidemiology of Body Dysmorphic Disorder among Adolescents: A Study of Their Cognitive Functions," published in the March 22, 2022, volume of *Brain Behavior*, found that a significant percentage of people with body dysmorphic disorder have distorted perceptions of their bodies because they have visual-spatial processing deficits. The upshot: we need more research to distinguish NVLD from other disorders with the goal of developing interventions specifically for NVLDers.

John

John doesn't have any visible physical limitations, but he's on the autism spectrum. He has difficulty with eye contact and expressing his emotions and speaks in a monotone voice. Like many people on the spectrum, John has an area of interest that he knows inside and out: trains. He knows the entire New York City subway system like the back of his hand and can tell you instantly how to get to where you're going. He talks about trains frequently, but his communication is one-sided and nonreciprocal, as though he is a professor giving a lecture that no one cares to hear.

People usually tolerate his odd behaviors and do not hold him accountable for his lack of knowledge of social-emotional skills because his limitations are clear. In his work with computers, he's a virtual genius and makes a very good living. Sometimes when John gets overwhelmed, he calms himself by "stimming" (self-stimulating behaviors that usually involve repetitive movements or sounds) and flapping his arms. He has learned how to excuse himself and go to a quiet location where he can calm down. Unlike Danielle, John has coworkers who understand and accept him.

Billy

Over the years, I began to keep a journal about those students who just didn't seem to fit the labels they were assigned. My intuition, along with my personal experiences, led me to believe there was more to some of these students than was meeting the eye—as was the case with me.

Billy was a student in my special education class. He had a learning disability that caused him difficulties in perceiving and processing information. He lagged behind his peers in math and had trouble socializing with his classmates.

One day during class, Billy was playing with something under his desk. I couldn't see what it was, but it was capturing the interest of the students around him and interrupting my lesson. I asked Billy to put away whatever it was and told him that he could share it with the class during free time. It wasn't long before Billy took it out of his desk and began to sneakily show it to the other kids.

Giving him the opportunity once again to redeem himself, I said, "Billy, would you mind bringing me whatever it is you have?"

Billy said, "No, I don't want to give it to you."

Later, in private, I asked Billy why he said no when I told him to bring it to me. He explained by saying that I didn't *tell* him to give it to me; I *asked* him to. I explained to him that although I didn't directly tell him by the *words* I said, that was what I *meant* and that I thought he knew that and, therefore, wasn't following my directions. Billy then said, as if he were the teacher and I were the student, that I should have said that in the first place!

Had this happened with another teacher, Billy would have lost recess, been given after-school detention, or have been sent to the principal's office for giving a fresh or smart-aleck response. I had a feeling that Billy wasn't looking for trouble or being intentionally disruptive, even though that was his reputation with the other teachers in the school. Since there had been similar situations like this in the past with Billy, and this had happened to me as a kid, I began to investigate further.

I discovered that Billy truly didn't think he was disobeying me. He was only able to understand the *literal* meaning of the words. He could not understand by the tone of my voice, my gesture of pointing to what he was playing with, or my strong eye contact and facial expressions that it wasn't a choice, and I was expecting him to bring the item to me. This is a classic example of NVLD—*being unable to understand the meaning of verbal communication because of an inability to interpret nonverbal communication.*

Falling through the Cracks

Mallory's daughter, Jackie, was diagnosed with NVLD in grade school by a neuropsychologist, as some diagnosticians do recognize NVLD, despite it not being in the *DSM*. Mallory, being aware of the differences of opinions among professionals, was careful in selecting a neuropsychologist for Jackie's upcoming reevaluation. In preparation, she interviewed several professionals to find one who was in favor of confirming Jackie's NVLD diagnosis. Instead of receiving the expected outcome, it was determined she did not have NVLD, and she was diagnosed as being on the autistic spectrum.

Mallory was confused, so it was only natural for her to question the results. The psychologist told her that when she did make the diagnosis in the past, it was because, in her previous workplace, she had been instructed to support and acknowledge the diagnosis of NVLD in her evaluations. But now, being in her private practice, she had the freedom to make decisions on her own. She explained that in her opinion, NVLD doesn't exist, as it's not recognized in the *DSM*.

Unlike other learning disabilities, NVLD isn't covered under the Individuals with Disabilities Education Act (IDEA). So, even with a formal diagnosis, your child may not qualify for an individualized education plan (IEP) or 504 plan from their school unless they have another diagnosis or disability that is recognized. Mallory is in a catch-22 situation, as she needs the NVLD diagnosis so the professionals working with Jackie can better help her.

Despite the overlap in symptoms with autism, not all of the same interventions would help, though some would. However, if Mallory doesn't accept the diagnosis of autism, her daughter is in jeopardy of not receiving school services.

NVLD Checklists

The following lists identify the characteristics and deficits common among children and adults with NVLD. Not everyone will have all these difficulties, and some may even excel in some of these areas. Keep in mind that this list isn't meant to be exhaustive. It is designed to help you identify traits and patterns you have seen in your child or experienced yourself. Check all the characteristics that apply to you or your child.

Providing a copy of this checklist and the results of the quizzes to a diagnostician can be helpful. A comprehensive neuropsychological assessment by a skilled clinician experienced in NVLD is the only way to receive a diagnosis—so any information you can provide the clinician is important.

Visual-Spatial and Motor Skills

- knowing where your body is in relation to spaces and surroundings
- identifying where objects are in relation to each other in the environment
- using fine motor skills, such as cutting with scissors, tying shoes, and handwriting
- bumping into things or getting hurt easily
- visually discriminating and finding objects in front of you
- coordinating movements and following sequenced dance or exercise steps
- being labeled "clumsy" or always getting in the way
- invading others' personal space by standing too close
- getting lost when driving or finding your way around in buildings
- learning how to drive
- judging far and near distances
- catching and throwing a ball
- swimming and riding a bike
- opening doors with locks
- using hands-on equipment
- eating with utensils
- falling out of chairs and furniture
- walking a straight line
- playing sports
- writing legibly

- interpreting charts and graphs
- understanding concepts
- visualizing
- knowing left from right
- telling time on an analog clock
- discriminating between objects and shapes
- completing puzzles
- identifying differences between objects
- remembering images

Academics
- solving math problems
- counting on fingers
- counting by odd or even numbers
- counting money and making change
- confusing visual signs (e.g., add, subtract, multiply, divide)
- copying from the board
- reading comprehension
- organization of writing
- critical or higher-order thinking

Social-Emotional Communication and Behavior
- interpreting tone of voice and identifying sarcasm
- oversharing
- recognizing when someone is leading you on

- recognizing nonverbal cues (facial expressions, body language, emotions, posture)
- needing to verbally label information in order to understand it
- exhibiting unintentionally inappropriate behavior
- reciprocal communication
- having rigid, inflexible thinking
- understanding how you present yourself to others
- generalizing social information and concepts for a variety of situations
- social problem-solving and repairing relationships
- looking to others for affirmation
- experiencing bullying
- understanding jokes
- interpreting figurative language, such as metaphors, idioms, and hyperbole
- comprehending implied meanings and reading between the lines
- getting along with others
- struggling with mental health, including depression, anxiety, and co-occurring conditions
- asking too many questions, to the point of being repetitive or interrupting the regular flow of conversation
- overreacting
- finding transitions and changes challenging
- expressing thoughts in blunt, tactless language

Executive Functioning
- organizing and planning
- prioritizing
- managing time
- initiating tasks
- adjusting behavior to unexpected or novel situations
- controlling and regulating emotions
- focusing
- using working memory

NVLD Strengths
Typically, those with NVLD have the following strengths in common:
- verbal intelligence
- verbal expression
- rote memory
- fluency in reading
- spelling
- broad range of information and knowledge
- strong vocabulary
- empathy
- public speaking
- research

Parent Screening: Could Your Child Have NVLD?

Answer "yes" or "no" to the following questions:

1. Does your child socialize better with kids who are younger or older than his or her age?
2. Does your child become upset and say, "That's not what you said," and insist you said something else?
3. Does your child believe what others say as the truth? Is your child gullible, easily led, naive, or incapable of dishonesty?
4. Do you find yourself saying to your child, "I know that's what I said, but this is what I meant"?
5. Does your child interpret words at "face value" (i.e., literally)? Is your child unable to read between the lines?
6. Does your child have exceptional verbal skills but not always understand the meanings of words?
7. Does your child read fluently but struggle to comprehend and answer questions about what he or she read?
8. Does your child come off as rude, self-centered, inflexible, or bossy to others?
9. Are your child's social-emotional skills or maturity level below his or her age level?
10. Do you or others become frustrated by your child's seemingly endless barrage of questions?
11. Does your child have trouble making or keeping friends?
12. Does your child experience bullying, or is he or she excluded by peers?

13. Does your child tend to learn about activities and birthday parties after the fact, not having been invited?
14. Does your child struggle with knowing when someone is joking or being sarcastic?
15. Does your child have trouble using scissors, zippers, and buttons or with writing, tying shoes, or participating in sports?
16. Does your child become upset with new environments, teasing, or changes in schedule?
17. Is your child blunt, honest to a fault, or unaware of hurting someone's feelings? Does your child know what is inappropriate to say to others?
18. Does your child have "all or nothing thinking" or see things as only black or white?
19. Does your child have trouble understanding any of the following: slang, abstract concepts, idioms, tone of voice, body language, or facial expressions?
20. Does your child struggle to manage social situations?
21. Does your child struggle with balance, coordination, bumping into and dropping things, dancing, learning how to swim or ride a bike, or participating in sports?
22. Does your child have trouble reading body language, facial expressions, gestures, or tone of voice?
23. Does your child isolate themselves from others?
24. Does your child read or do other activities when with others to avoid social interactions?
25. Does your child struggle with math?

26. Does your child have trouble writing on the lines?
27. Does your child have difficulty with thinking and comprehending beyond factual information?

If you answered yes to seven or more of these questions, you may want your child to be evaluated for NVLD.

NVLD Screening for Adolescents and Adults: Could You Have NVLD?

Answer each question without overthinking it. Circle the answer that best applies.

1. Do you get the details but have trouble putting them together to understand the big picture?
   - very often
   - often
   - sometimes
   - rarely
   - never

2. Do you get lost easily or rely on GPS even to go to a place you have been before?
   - very often
   - often
   - sometimes
   - rarely
   - never

3. Do you have difficulties reading maps or interpreting diagrams, graphs, or charts?
   - very often
   - often
   - sometimes
   - rarely
   - never

4. Do you have difficulty with math skills and concepts?
   - very often
   - often
   - sometimes
   - rarely
   - never

5. Do you overshare personal information?
   - very often
   - often
   - sometimes
   - rarely
   - never

6. Do you give too many details or explain too much when talking to someone?
   - very often
   - often
   - sometimes
   - rarely
   - never

7. Do you need to ask a lot of questions to understand what people are saying?
   - very often
   - often
   - sometimes
   - rarely
   - never

8. Do others become annoyed with you for asking too many questions?
   - very often
   - often
   - sometimes
   - rarely
   - never

9. Do others tell you that you don't listen or to stop interrupting them?
   - very often
   - often
   - sometimes
   - rarely
   - never

10. Do you bump into people or objects, drop things, or get hurt easily?
    - very often
    - often
    - sometimes
    - rarely
    - never

11. Do you feel you are easily led or gullible?
    - very often
    - often
    - sometimes
    - rarely
    - never

12. Do you get upset when others tease you?
    - very often
    - often
    - sometimes
    - rarely
    - never

13. Do you have difficulty learning how to play cards or board games?
    - very often
    - often
    - sometimes
    - rarely
    - never

14. Do you have difficulty with any of the following: using scissors, fixing or operating equipment/household items, buttoning, zipping, or breaking things unintentionally?
    - very often
    - often
    - sometimes
    - rarely
    - never

15. Do you struggle or did it take you longer than others to learn how to swim, ride a bike, participate in sports, or walk in a straight line?
    - very often
    - often
    - sometimes
    - rarely
    - never

16. Do you nod your head to convey you are understanding what others are saying when, in fact, you don't understand?
    - very often
    - often
    - sometimes
    - rarely
    - never

17. Do others say you take things too literally or think differently?
    - very often
    - often
    - sometimes
    - rarely
    - never

18. Do you find it difficult to organize your thoughts when writing?
    - very often
    - often
    - sometimes
    - rarely
    - never

19. Do you read fluently but struggle to answer questions about or comprehend what you have you read?
    - very often
    - often
    - sometimes
    - rarely
    - never

20. Do you pretend to understand jokes and laugh, even when you don't get them?
    - very often
    - often
    - sometimes
    - rarely
    - never

21. Do you struggle with handwriting?
    - very often
    - often
    - sometimes
    - rarely
    - never

22. Do you have trouble making friends or have trouble keeping them?
    - very often
    - often
    - sometimes
    - rarely
    - never

23. Do you feel you are excluded from social activities?
    - very often
    - often
    - sometimes
    - rarely
    - never

24. Do you have social anxiety or depression?
    - very often
    - often
    - sometimes
    - rarely
    - never

25. Do you have difficulty with thinking and comprehending beyond factual information?
    - very often
    - often
    - sometimes
    - rarely
    - never

26. Do you seek approval and direction from others?
    - very often
    - often
    - sometimes
    - rarely
    - never

27. Do you have trouble recognizing and understanding nonverbal communication cues (facial expressions, body language, emotions, posture)?
    - very often
    - often
    - sometimes
    - rarely
    - never

If you answered "very often" nine or more times, you may want to be evaluated for NVLD.

Chapter 2

Is It You, Me, or NVLD?

Throughout my childhood and early adult years, my parents, teachers, friends, and others would get mad at me for the things I did without knowing any better. Thankfully, before my diagnosis, I had figured out ways to not only cope but remediate some of my difficulties, which I'll talk about later on in the book.

People were often puzzled by my responses and reactions, which seemed off base compared to what actually happened or to what was being communicated. This led them to think I was not listening. Much later, my parents understood and felt bad for not knowing I wasn't intentionally misbehaving. The root cause was my inability to interpret and process nonverbal communication.

Just like you can't read without learning the alphabet, you can't understand what others are communicating without interpreting nonverbal cues. Reading nonverbal communication isn't a subject taught in school. It's assumed that most people learn nonverbal and social communication automatically and intuitively through visual observation and role-modeling of others, a process that begins in early childhood and continues throughout the school years.

One of the things I really struggled with was reading facial expressions that were neutral—also referred to as a "resting face"—and showed very little to no emotion. Unlike my peers, I wasn't able to intuitively and effortlessly gauge a person's mood, the setting, or the situation and adjust my behavioral responses accordingly. My mind was flooded with endless questions I couldn't answer. Did I do something wrong? Are they mad at me? Why am I being ignored? Am I wanted here? Should I stay or leave? What happened? What did they mean when they said that? What should I have done instead?

When I couldn't figure out what had happened or what was expected of me, I assumed I was responsible for the feelings of others and blamed myself. It was easier to withdraw socially than to be misunderstood. It's like being told the color you see as red is blue. I lived with chronic anxiety, feeling as if the ground beneath my feet was unstable and shaky, as if I were walking on Jell-O.

Many times, when I asked my mother if she was mad at me, she would say, "No." After some time passed and I still couldn't figure out what was going on, I would ask again, "Are you sure you're not mad at me?" This cycle would repeat itself. Each time, I would change the words, but, essentially, I was just asking the same thing over and over again in different ways. When she asked me, "Why do you think I'm mad?" I would give her a list of reasons: "You're not talking to me; you sounded angry; you said this, or you didn't say that…" I could be relentless and get on her last nerve until she was at her wit's end! When she finally reached her breaking point, she would yell at me to stop asking her. Once I understood she was not upset about me or about a specific issue, I'd calm down.

Tiptoe through the Tulips

Have you ever heard the popular 1960s song "Tiptoe through the Tulips" by Tiny Tim? It was so unexpected and entertaining to see this big, yet childlike, eccentric (possibly neurodivergent) man with long curly hair playing a small ukulele and singing in falsetto. If you've never seen or heard of him, you can check him out on YouTube and come to your own conclusions.

Tiny Tim's strange voice may have made some people cringe but not as much as my mom cringed when I brought her some tulips. Mom was from the Netherlands, and like most Dutch people, she loved flowers, especially tulips. Whenever I would hear Tim's song, it reminded me of my mother and her precious tulips.

One day, I chopped the heads off some tulips in her garden and put them in a bowl of water. When Mom said, "Oh, I see you picked my tulips?" I was only able to understand her verbal communication literally. She did not say she was angry, and I didn't understand from her nonverbal communication that cutting the heads off of tulips was verboten. When she asked why I picked them, I told her I knew she liked tulips, and I wanted to give them to her. She told me she liked seeing them growing in the ground, but she put the bowls of tulip tops around the house, adding that she would just have to enjoy them this way now.

In my world, we were good! In hers, she was being kind and making the best of it. If I had been able to decipher her nonverbal communication, I would have known she was not a happy camper. I was at an age where she expected me to comprehend nonverbal cues—to know that when someone crosses their arms on their chest, moves their eyes upward, and says, "What did you do?" in a frustrated tone of voice while shaking their head back and forth, it means that the person is not happy with what you did, and therefore you should not do it again!

Can you picture what happened the next day when I finished the job off, cutting the remaining tulips in the backyard, thinking once again I was doing something nice for her? This time, I was reprimanded and punished for my poor behavior. I felt ashamed. No matter how many times I told her I didn't understand and didn't know what I was doing was wrong, she wanted to hear nothing about it.

Now I realize this sounds like a funny story, but I want you to really think about this. Can you imagine if your parents, teachers, bosses, spouse, friends, and others continually became upset with you, and you had no idea why or what you did to cause this? Scenarios like this happen at all ages to those with NVLD. You or your child may get defensive, angry, anxious, or depressed. Each time this happens, you fall further into a deep black hole—that is, until you get the right kind of help and begin to find your way out!

Chris Rock

I started this book at the beginning of the pandemic. Being quarantined provided the time and opportunity for self-reflection and starting things that I had long kept on the back burner—so too for comedian and actor Chris Rock. He has shared that he spent so much time alone as a result of COVID-19 that he began thinking about what he could find in his life that would give him joy from just getting up every morning.

Chris Rock dropped out of school to pursue comedy because he felt it was the first thing he was ever good at. He always knew something was off about himself but didn't know what. One of his friends suggested he may have Asperger's. It was then he reached out for help and completed nine hours of testing, which revealed he had NVLD.

Chris explains that he misunderstands most nonverbal communication. Like others with NVLD, he interprets words literally. He had never understood others' negative reactions to him and assumed they were due to the fact that he was "famous." "Whenever someone would respond to me in a negative way, I'd think,

'Whatever, they're responding to something that has to do with who they think I am.' Now, I'm realizing it was me. A lot of it was me."[1]

Many people with NVLD have difficulty learning how to swim, ride a bike, and play sports because of visual-spatial and visual-motor deficits. At the age of fifty-five, Chris Rock decided to learn to swim. He has said, "Do you know how f*** hard it is for a grown-up to learn how to swim? You've got to not be scared to die."

I'm extremely grateful to Chris for his bravery in sharing his diagnosis and his struggles in public. Having the support of a well-known public figure benefits the NVLD community by raising awareness on a national level and aiding as an official disorder (classified in the *DSM*), which will aid in increasing research funding, understanding, acceptance, treatment and support.

---

[1] (Rose, Lacey. "'This Is the Best Part I've Ever Had': Chris Rock Talks 'Fargo,' Aging and Why He's Spending 7 Hours a Week in Therapy." The Hollywood Reporter, 16 September 2020. https://www.hollywoodreporter.com/movies/movie-features/this-is-the-best-part-ive-ever-had-how-chris-rocks-extensive-therapy-helped-prepare-him-for-fargo-4060631/).

Misunderstanding Madness

Communication can be frustrating and confusing on a daily basis for those with NVLD. The degree varies in intensity depending on the situation, expectations, and circumstances. The stress of continual misinterpretations effects how others perceive us. The shame and embarrassment about being judged, labeled, ridiculed, and misunderstood contributes to underachievement, low self-esteem, and lack of self-confidence. Once or twice isn't a big deal, but constant misinterpretation and rejections can lead to depression, anxiety, and feelings of hopelessness.

As Chris' experience demonstrates, when others repetitively respond negatively to yourself or your child, it's difficult to know the cause. You may be thinking, is it me or them? Now that you have this book, you may wonder, could there be another possibility - NVLD?

The 1930's comedy routine, "Who's on First," is a skit by Abbott and Costello that echoes the frustration between a neurotypical person and a neurodivergent person who are trying to communicate effectively with one another but can't. Read the excerpt from the script in the box below or, even better, watch it on YouTube to experience the full effect within the context of communication between NVLDers and NTs.

Who's On First
By Abbott and Costello

ABBOTT: Well Costello, I'm going to New York with you. You know Bucky Harris, the Yank's manager, gave me a job as coach for as long as you're on the team.

COSTELLO: Look, Abbott, if you're the coach, you must know all the players playing on the team.

ABBOTT: Oh, I'll tell you their names, but you know, strange as it may seem, they give these ball players, nowadays, very peculiar names.

COSTELLO: You mean funny names?

ABBOTT: Strange names, pet names. Like, Dizzy Dean, and…

ABBOTT: Daffy Dean.

COSTELLO: And their French cousin.

ABBOTT: French?

COSTELLO: Goofé.

ABBOTT: Goofé Dean, oh I see! Well, let's see, we have on the bags, Who's on first, What's on second, and I Don't Know is on third.

COSTELLO: That's what I want to find out.

ABBOTT: I say, Who's on first, What's on second, and I Don't Know's on third.

COSTELLO: Are you the manager?

ABBOTT: Yes.

COSTELLO: You gonna be the coach too?
ABBOTT: Yes.
COSTELLO: And you don't know the fellows' names?
ABBOTT: Well, I should.
COSTELLO: Well then, who's on first?
ABBOTT: Yes.
COSTELLO: I mean the fellow's name.
ABBOTT: Who.
COSTELLO: The guy on first.
ABBOTT: Who.
COSTELLO: The first baseman.
ABBOTT: Who!
COSTELLO: The guy playing first base.
ABBOTT: Who is on first.
COSTELLO: I'm asking you who's on first!
ABBOTT: That's the man's name.
COSTELLO: That's who's name?
ABBOTT: Yeah.
COSTELLO: Well, go ahead and tell me.
ABBOTT: That's it.
COSTELLO: That's who?
ABBOTT: Yeah. (Pause)
COSTELLO: Look, you gotta first baseman?
ABBOTT: Certainly.
COSTELLO: Who's playing first?
ABBOTT: That's right.

> COSTELLO: When you pay off the first baseman every month, who gets the money?
> ABBOTT: Every dollar of it.
> COSTELLO: All I'm trying to find out is the fellow's name on first base…

Survival Mode: Asking Questions

In the last line, Costello says, "All I'm trying to do is to find out the fellow's name on first base." Just like Costello, I'd ask my dad so many questions sometimes he'd get annoyed with me and say, "What, are you a detective?" When NVLDers have trouble grasping what others are saying, they may interrupt and question them to get the words they desperately need for comprehension. This can be a frustrating experience for both the speaker and listener, causing them to become irritated with each other. I got in trouble many times when others interpreted my need to ask questions as me being difficult. In reality, I was merely trying to get information I needed to understand what they were saying.

If you were blind, you could learn how to navigate your environment by memorizing the placement of furniture and other essential items. But what if someone moved the furniture and you couldn't find your way around? Scary, right? Left to your own devices and without assistance from others, the stress would most likely cause you to become extremely anxious. What if every time you finally figured out the new placement, the furniture was moved again? To compensate for these changes and lack of sight, you would most likely ask questions to verbally receive the information you need to find your way.

Yet, unlike those without sight, NVLDers are denied the patience of others when they need assistance. Many have reported to me that while they are just trying to understand, their questions have caused others to feel overwhelmed, challenged, or disbelieved. Exasperated, they may give up trying to explain, tell the NVLDer to just trust them, and end the conversation. If the questions don't stop, NVLDers may be accused of being argumentative or not trusting that what the other person says is true. In reality, nothing could be further from the truth.

Most people expect others to listen until they are finished speaking before asking questions. If you, an NVLDer, do not tell others your communication style in advance, they will assume you are being rude. Moreover, it's not always possible for someone with NVLD, as well as those with ADHD and auditory-processing disorders, to wait until the speaker is finished before asking questions. Their brains need more time to process and understand the initial information, assimilate new information, and fill in the gaps. Many will need to ask questions before the person has finished speaking. Waiting until the end leaves them more lost, confused, and embarrassed than if they had been able to process the information in chunks along the way.

To help yourself or your child, role-play a conversation where you prepare the person you will be talking to in advance by saying, "I process language differently so I may need to stop you when you are in the middle of speaking to be sure I comprehend what you're saying or to clarify by asking you questions. You may feel as if I am not listening or am being rude. Be assured it's none of these things. I just want to make sure we understand one another so I can respond appropriately."

Reflective Listening and Communication

There will be times when you'll need to ask close-ended questions to get the facts you need. However, you'll also need to incorporate reflective listening (RL) skills into your communications strategy toolbox.

RL is not based on asking questions, but rather clarifying what someone is expressing (needs, beliefs, feelings). This is done by repeating to the person what they said in your own words. If you have not understood them, they can clarify what they said for you. RL makes for harmonious communication and will improve your relationships. It's an excellent tool for NVLDers of all ages.

Communication Connections

Prior to being diagnosed with NVLD, many people often either chalk up the negative responses of others to them as isolated incidents or take on the blame for a specific issue themselves. In other words, they don't know that their difficulties processing communication may be the cause of the negative responses.

Over time, most NVLDers will figure out the miscommunication connection from the frequency of their conflicts with different people in unrelated environments. They may become introspective and start their own research into NVLD. They may self-diagnose, reach out for help from others, seek a professional evaluation, or receive feedback from close friends or family members.

Lessons Learned

- Think about difficult conversations you've had in various environments with different people. Can you make connections between times when you misunderstood others or they misunderstood you? Identify the skills you need to improve upon based on these experiences.
- Role-play these situations with a trusted friend, practicing what you could do differently.
- Practice inconspicuous breathing techniques to stay calm when misunderstood in the present moment.
- Rehearse prepared one-liners to use when communication challenges come up, such as "I know that this might seem off topic but…" or "Thank you for sharing that with me. Do you mind if I take a minute or two to think about it before I respond?"

- Ask questions but know when to stop.
- Use reflective listening.
- When frustrated, excuse yourself politely and take the time to decompress and strategize before returning.
- Use email for easier communication.

Chapter 3

The Home Front

My parents met when their paths crossed during World War II. My grandfather was part of the Dutch resistance working underground to save Jewish people during the Holocaust. He would often invite soldiers he met to his house to play cards. My dad, a medic during the war, was one of those soldiers. He didn't speak Dutch, and my mom didn't speak English, but they somehow learned to communicate with one another. Neither of my parents had the opportunity to graduate high school because of the war. Unbeknownst to them, they would be raising children with neurodiversity, which may have seemed like living through another type of war. They were happily married for seventy-five years.

My dad was my biggest fan growing up and continued to be until his passing during the writing of this book. He had many of the same difficulties during his school years as I had. Although it was very different back then—Dad was just shy of one hundred years of age when he passed—he understood my challenges firsthand. I always suspected my dad had NVLD. He excelled in his career, thanks to his excellent verbal skills, which is typical of those with NVLD.

Dad spent a lot of time explaining things to me to help me cope with my difficulties. It was his great sense of humor and storytelling skills, along with his unconditional love, that built up my confidence. He taught me ways to work around my challenges. I never got in trouble for poor grades. He would ask me if I did the best I could, and that was good enough in his eyes. Even though I always had tutors, I continued to struggle, especially in math, which is difficult for those with NVLD.

In contrast, my mother was a nervous wreck since she didn't know how to help me. She was so worried about my future as an adult. How would I take care of myself financially and fit in socially?

My mother scheduled my time with tutors, Girl Scouts, and dancing, guitar, and art classes. In dance class, I had trouble learning the steps. It didn't matter in the beginning because young kids are cute when they don't know the steps, but as I got older, it became so embarrassing and painful that I had to quit. Mom didn't know that my visual-spatial difficulties caused me problems with coordination, balance, and dyspraxia (also known as developmental coordination disorder), which made me stick out like a sore thumb. Had there been an awareness of social-emotional skills and learning executive functioning interventions back then, I would have been able to bypass some of the pain I experienced.

Mom did anything she could to help me make friends and do well in school. When it became apparent that I wouldn't be able to play the piano or guitar or dance, my mother did not give up. She continued to explore other avenues, providing me with opportunities to be successful at something, which turned out to be acting classes. These classes proved to be invaluable to me as you will learn more about in the friendship chapter.

My parents knew I was gullible and easily led, as is common with NVLD. They didn't know the causes, but they knew I was not as mature as other kids my age. As a result, they became overprotective of me, and rightly so, to ensure I would be safe from others. As they discovered from my adventure with the tulips, I misunderstood most of what was said to me, largely because I took everything literally. What they didn't understand was the cause: NVLD

Literal Linda, Lazy Linda

During my middle school years, my parents wouldn't let me hang out at night with the other kids at playgrounds or in front of the 7-Eleven store and other outdoor places. When I repeatedly wouldn't accept no for an answer, my frustrated father explained, "You don't want to go out at night; that's when all the crumbs, bad people, come out and do bad things." Taking this to heart, I would stay up all night, frozen in my bed from fear, afraid to sleep. I thought each sound I heard meant that someone was trying to break in. I had to go to bed with the lights on and would only fall asleep when the sun came up in the morning. This left me with only an hour or two of sleep, so I was exhausted while at school. My dad's desire to help me to understand why he was not allowing me out at night led him to use an example that had long-lasting consequences for me.

My parents were also frustrated with my knee-jerk reactions and outbursts. They thought I was being overly dramatic and was making things up. One time, an older kid told me that he was going to hang another kid upside down by his toenails and torture him. Although I was at an age where I should have understood he was joking, I took his words literally because he was saying it as if he was serious. I became frantic he would do it to me too if I ever upset him.

Mike, one of my kindergarten students, became upset when his mom said it was raining cats and dogs outside. He was inconsolable because he thought his mom was lying since he didn't see any cats or dogs coming down from the sky with the rain. He was worried that if this happened, they would get hurt. Even after his mother explained, he kept on saying, "That's not what you said." Although the scenarios vary by age, such situations occur with those of all ages with NVLD. If you frequently find yourself thinking, "Yes, that's what I said, but it's not what I meant," it's likely that this person may have NVLD.

My mother would get *sooooo* angry with me for the way I kept my room. An extremely organized person, she had no point of reference for just how difficult it was for me. No matter how hard I tried, I could never please her. She didn't understand the cause was poor executive functioning skills resulting from NVLD and ADHD.

My room, with bits and pieces of things all over the place, looked like a nuclear bomb had exploded in it. I never knew where any of my things were because I didn't have the focus and patience to sort through my belongings and put them away. Moreover, I didn't have the visual memory to know where the clothes belonged when putting them away. I couldn't consistently keep them neatly organized in the same way and order. I needed to see things in front of me to know where they were. My visual discrimination was so poor I could be looking for my shoes and not be able to find them among others in my closet, even if they were right in front of me. My mother was exasperated.

Many parents and partners of those with NVLD and ADHD are unable to wrap their heads around how their children or significant others are unable to organize their things. One parent I worked with found a year-old salad underneath her teenage daughter's bed! It's even harder for those parents and partners who have good organizational skills because they can't relate and may see the disorder as laziness. Some are unable to alter their expectations or assist their loved ones in learning how to better manage themselves. They don't mean to be callous; just like my mother, they are frustrated.

How My Parents Helped Me
I wasn't coddled, and I grew up in a time where there were fewer distractions. Having only a few channels to watch on TV and a rotary phone—no email, smartphones, apps, YouTube,

texting, or online gaming—really kept me grounded in the present moment. I didn't have the immediate gratification or the disconnection that can come from the stimulation-response feedback loop created by today's technology. As a result, I felt most of my feelings rather than blocking and numbing them by using the internet.

Being in the present moment wasn't always fun; it was painful dealing with disappointments and setbacks, but it was also necessary for my continual growth. I benefited greatly from the things my father taught me. They were life lessons, tools I could rely on throughout the different stages of my life. I am grateful that my parents trusted their instincts, accepted me for who I was, and loved and supported me unconditionally, despite all the misunderstandings

Lessons from My Father
Resilience

My parents expected me to work hard and to keep trying if things didn't work out. They carefully considered my requests for help, and if they did help me out, I appreciated it. I wasn't treated like a fragile piece of china that could break at any moment. They weren't concerned if I was happy or unhappy with them, and they didn't need to be my friends. I learned to cope and to persevere when things were tough.

I see many parents who feel sorry for their learning-disabled kids. Their thinking goes something like this: "School is such a hard place that we want to make home a safe haven." They set the bar too low and adjust their expectations by giving their children what they want and not holding them accountable for their actions. Those children then go out into the real world with unrealistic expectations and unequipped to cope and manage on their own when things don't go their way.

One of the most important things I learned was that I could struggle, and I would survive. It wasn't the end of the world. Life can have painful aspects and still be worth living.

Entrepreneurship

My dad supported me in starting my own business to provide services for ND students that weren't offered by the schools. Not only did my dad believe in my mission, he had no doubt that I would be successful on my own.

Being Different Is OK

I was shaped by how my dad looked at me. He didn't know about neurodivergence; he just knew I was different. Dad accepted me for who I was and turned my differences into positives. He was ahead of his time.

No Judgment

Dad always told me I was not a "run-of-the-mill Millie." He embraced my uniqueness as an asset, not a liability. He praised my impulsivity and said, "That's my Linda," always one step ahead of the game! He accepted who I was without judgment. This encouraged me and created a space where I could view myself optimistically, which gave me the confidence to venture out and take risks.

Black and White Equals Gray

NVLDers may think in terms of black and white and struggle to see the gray. They can be rigid thinkers and are often unable to discern nuances. My dad coined his own phrases and used them to teach me. When I struggled, he verbally broke things down for me, which helped me adjust my thinking.

You Had to Be There

The idiom "you had to be there" was one of my dad's famous sayings, which he used when I was struggling to understand and interpret things that had happened in my absence. Sometimes I learned that it had nothing to do with me misunderstanding others. We truly don't know what happened or can't appreciate conversations unless we are present when they transpire. Using idioms with your child is a way to teach higher-level thinking skills.

What Did You Learn from That?

Dad never discouraged me from experiencing and exploring new things, even if he thought I might not succeed. He allowed me to try things for myself, and he allowed me to fail. He didn't step in and put out my fires. Each time things didn't work out the way I had hoped, he would ask me, "What did you learn from that?" He impressed upon me that I didn't fail, and therefore, I wasn't a failure. Not meeting my goals or expectations exposed me to new learning. He taught me how to reflect and see the lessons in the situations.

Talking and Problem-Solving

My dad and I talked a lot. In his infinite wisdom, before we even knew about NVLD, he discovered that I needed to talk things through and have unwritten social rules explained to me. He taught me how to process and review my interactions with others. I was not always able to follow and understand conversations. He was able to turn the abstract and unknown into something concrete I could understand. As he did this repeatedly, it actually trained my brain and helped me to understand social norms and to develop interpersonal skills.

Keep It Simple

Dad's philosophy was don't make it so complicated. Don't make it harder. Do what works, and don't feel bad about it. If it works for you, then it's good enough. He used the analogy of baking a cake. Sure, some people are going to go all out and make a seven-layer cake from scratch with homemade frosting, but a simple yellow cake from the box is going to be just as sweet!

Empathy and Learning

Since he, too, had difficulties in school, he was patient with me. He showed me empathy by telling me stories about the difficulties he had in school. I was able to see that I did not have to base my self-worth on academic success. We now know that the most important predictor of life success is social skills. Would you rather have a mentally healthy child getting B's or C's or a straight-A student crippled with depression, anxiety, and low self-worth? He taught me that I am a person, not a grade. A grade doesn't measure a person or the success they can achieve. The individual who launched FedEx wrote an economics paper about how the delivery of "express goods" could be expedited into the US delivery system—for which he received a C-. I am sure he's happy he didn't take that C- as an accurate measure of his idea!

Gratitude and Meditation

Long before gratitude and meditation were in fashion, my dad taught me how to appreciate the little things in life. For instance, he was happy just to have a nice steak for dinner. He would say to me, "Look at the sky, the clouds, and the water. Meditate on that, and appreciate the beauty." When I would get down on myself and become depressed, he would point these things out to me as a reminder to be grateful and mindful of the present moment.

Don't Burn Your Bridges, and Keep the Doors Open

Being literal and taking words at face value can make NVLDers at times come across as cantankerous. Misinterpreting situations, they may think others have intentionally said or done something to invalidate them. They may appear defensive and lash out at others in an attempt to protect themselves, which damages their relationships. NVLDers are also targets for other people who do not understand their challenges and may think less of them or put them down.

Nonetheless, my dad taught me the importance of not burning my bridges because you never know when you may need that person. Another way he put this was "Keep your doors open." Never close doors on relationships, no matter how mad you get, as closed doors limit opportunities.

When I shared with him what someone had done to me, he would say in a singsong voice, "Don't burn your bridges, and keep your doors open." To further illustrate, he would pretend to open a closed door. When he closed it, he would say something negative that would keep the door closed or burn the bridge and end the relationship. When he pretended to open the door, he would say something productive to open the door and prevent the bridge from burning. Through this, I learned how to repair relationships rather than burn bridges.

Stay on the Path

When I wanted to give up, my dad would remind me to stay on the path. That meant to keep walking in the direction I wanted to go, toward the goal I wanted to reach.

What is important is that you stay on the path. Even though it's scary, and you don't know what's to come, you still have to go down the path if you want to achieve your goals. You don't have to know how to get from point A to point Z. You just need to take the next step. Each step will take you closer to where you want to be. You don't know how many miles the path is, or if the path is straight, steep, rocky, or curvy. Take each day as it comes, don't look too far ahead, and put one foot in front of the other. Along the way, you will discover what you need to do to get to the next step.

Chapter 4

School Daze:
Why Can't I Be Like Everyone Else?

My challenges started on the first day of kindergarten. I never seemed to fit in—no matter how hard I tried. School was really painful for me, academically and socially. There was very little awareness of ADHD and learning difficulties, let alone NVLD. Since I was a quiet and compliant student, I slipped through the cracks.

In kindergarten, I had no idea how to join in with the other kids. I vividly remember watching the other children play house. The girls imitated their mothers by pretending to cook, clean, and vacuum, while the boys mimicked their fathers by pretending to fix things around the house. My way of playing was to do what came naturally to me—talking. I proceeded to simply explain each step of how to make manicotti from scratch as I did with my mother. Of course, the other kids didn't want a play-by-play narrative of how to cook!

Not knowing what else to do, I would try to talk to the teacher on playground duty and attempt to make conversation about my mom's trip to her homeland or other things that were going on with my family. Having no interest whatsoever, she would tell me to go play with the other kids.

As I look back, my experiences make complete sense. Being unable to process nonverbal communication and interact through play and imitation, I navigated my world through words. Just like eyeglasses help others to see, I compensated by using my exceptional verbal skills—by "overtalking" my way through situations. This is typical for most people with NVLD.

A Deer in the Headlights

I couldn't always comprehend social situations or follow the conversations that went along with them. I was never sure of where I was supposed to be, what I should be doing or saying, and how I should act when I was with others. I was like a deer frozen in the headlights. This caused me tremendous anxiety—so much that I continued to suck my thumb while hiding out in the bathroom and when teachers had us put our heads down on our desks. At home, I continued to use my baby blanket around the house. My thumb became so raw and chapped that my parents used a remedy from the drugstore, painting on a liquid that tasted bad, to deter me. I also began to uncontrollably bite my nails to the point of bleeding and pain.

I felt so lonely, alone, and trapped in my own world as I watched other kids having fun and laughing. I didn't know what was wrong and thought, "Why can't I be like everyone else?" Day after day, my heart ached to join in, but I just didn't know how. The other kids didn't understand why I was sitting on the sidelines. To them, it looked like I wasn't interested in playing, so they ignored me.

Bullying in School

Kids intuitively know when someone is different, and bullies will zone in on those who are vulnerable. Like sharks in the water, they sense their prey. Typically, NT students have social ranking over children with NVLD and ND. The imbalance of power makes NDs more susceptible to bullying. Research indicates that children with disabilities are two to three times more likely to be bullied than their nondisabled peers.

In middle school, a group of "mean girls" led by my neighbor zoned in on me and made my life miserable. One time, they told me they were going to beat me up after school. I was terrified to walk home that day and told my homeroom teacher. She arranged with me that, at the end of the day, as we were packing up, she would say, in front of the class, that she wanted to see me after school. After everyone had left and the coast was clear, she drove me home.

I was so distraught by these episodes that my stomach began to ache. When these bullying incidents occurred, I took some Pepto Bismol. It was typical for me to go through a bottle of Pepto Bismol a week. My mother took me to the doctor, time and again. All the test results always came back negative, so the doctor concluded my stomach aches were the result of anxiety. Eventually, I was diagnosed with an ulcer. Soon after, I was too afraid to leave the house and became school phobic. Sometimes I pretended my stomach hurt even when it didn't. Feigning illness is a coping mechanism that children and adults with NVLD use to avoid painful experiences. The worst times were when the mean girls ganged up on me at school in places where there was little to no supervision, such as the lunchroom, the bathroom, the locker room, and on the playground.

The website Stopbullying.gov reports that students ages twelve to eighteen have experienced bullying in hallways and stairwells (43.4 percent), in classrooms (42.1 percent), in the cafeteria (26.8 percent), outside on school grounds (21.9 percent), online or through texting (15.3 percent), in the bathroom or locker room (12.1 percent), or somewhere else in the school building (2.1 percent)—places where kids are not protected and bullying is most likely to happen.

Parents Are Protection

Children with NVLD need to be protected in these hot spot school bullying zones. Become familiar with the bullying policies in your school district and your state. Keep your own notes, and be sure incidents are documented by the school with a follow-up plan of action as stipulated in these policies. Talk to your child's teacher and guidance counselor; they can team up to build a partnership between your child and with neurotypical "peer buddies" to level up their standing among other students. Peer buddies can help your child navigate these areas. Learn more about how to cope with bullying across the life span at Stopbullying.gov.

I didn't participate in extracurricular activities because I didn't fit in with any of the social groups—brains, popular crowd, artsy types, jocks, Goths, or the floaters who went from group to group. Fitting in is a major emotional need that intensifies during early adolescence. I was constantly looking for a way to be a part of one of these groups.

It's typical for NVLDers and NDs on the outskirts of their peers to gravitate toward other kids who are also on the outside of these cliques. These groups are composed of many different kids with a myriad of difficulties, including those with more severe difficulties. This can be the perfect storm for vulnerable and naive NVLDers, causing them to be in the wrong place at the wrong time and get into trouble.

Lucky for me I didn't get into trouble, but there were plenty of times I could have had I been caught during my rebellious high school years. I went along with the crowd as a follower to fit in. Keep a close eye on your child, as they may be too eager to please others and mimic inappropriate behaviors. By and large, they simply don't have street smarts, and because they desperately want friends, they can make poor judgments.

Humiliation

One of my middle school teachers wrote a sentence on the board that said, "She saw an elephant in the wild for the first time." When called on, I asked why it didn't say "a elephant" instead. Her response was "No, it's correct as 'an elephant' because the rule is you don't put two vowels next to each other in a sentence. Didn't you learn that in third and fourth grade?" This is one of the many reasons why I began to think I was stupid. I felt ashamed, ridiculed, belittled, and small, not least because a teacher made me feel that way.

No kid or adult wants to be singled out and criticized in front of others or be labeled as the one who always asks questions. Sooner or later, they will stop asking questions to avoid drawing attention to themselves. This is disastrous because the student doesn't understand what is being taught, is not able to follow along with lessons and directions, and thus does not learn important information. I can't tell you how many times I nodded my head and faked my way through classes, appearing to understand the instructor, because that is what NDs have to do to fit NTs' expectations of how people should communicate.

> ### Being an Advocate
>
> In addition to having strong parental support, children of all school ages need to learn to self-advocate. One of the things I tell my students to help them get through this is to talk to their teachers in private. Most are nervous, so to better prepare them, we practice this through role-play until they feel comfortable approaching the teacher. (Depending on the age of your student, you can modify suggestions I provided in chapter 2).

Ideally, learning to self-advocate begins in the elementary years. It's important to reinforce these skills for students throughout the school years. Once they are in college, their parents will not be able to run interference for them, as they are considered to be adults. It also helps to prepare them for the workforce, since some employees, new or otherwise, may need to speak to their bosses about the accommodations needed to perform their best on the job.

Learning Gaps

My inattentiveness, trouble staying on task, and weak executive functioning skills made learning difficult from kindergarten through college. As a result, I failed to master key information and basic concepts, such as when to use "a" and "an" in a sentence or things like identifying states on a map. My poor visual-spatial skills made discerning them by their shapes confusing.

Since I was not taught in the way I needed to learn, I was doing poorly in many classes and struggled to complete homework assignments and take tests. Many years later, these gaps in my education became a challenge for me because I had not mastered some of the basic skills I needed in the workplace. Later on in the book, you'll see how the consequences of this impacted me in the workforce.

As a classroom teacher, I used many different strategies and methods to prevent such learning gaps for my students. To help your child, I suggest that you start by identifying the gaps in your child's learning and then bring that information to the attention of school personnel. Ask to see the school's curriculum. Then look to see what your child does or does not know and add anything they still need to learn to their individualized education plan (IEP). If you're an adult, you can fill in the gaps and learn just about anything online with so many resources available.

Sports

Many NVLD kids and adults are unable to successfully participate in sports activities because of their poor visual-spatial skills. Volleyball, baseball, football, soccer, and field hockey require tracking the ball and judging its distance, reacting quickly while moving and coordinating the body simultaneously to connect with the ball. Many are kept from participating because no one wants them on their team.

My mom signed me up for a softball team. I hated it. I was terrified the ball would hit me, and I couldn't catch it to save my life, so other players had to leave their bases and catch the ball. I dreaded going up to bat. My mom wouldn't let me quit because she wanted me to learn to finish what I started. She gave me a pep talk and told me to do the best I could. Little did she know that when she dropped me off at practice, I would walk toward the field, wait until she pulled away, and then leave practice and go to a friend's house.

When Trying Harder Isn't the Answer

I wanted to do well, and I tried to meet the demands and expectations of a "good student." Homework was difficult since ADHD hindered my ability to focus. No matter how hard I tried, I just didn't "get" math—a common challenge for NVLDers. I was told that my handwriting was careless and sloppy because I wasn't trying hard enough, but that task is also a struggle for people with NVLD. Handwriting requires coordination of visual, spatial, and fine motor skills.

When trying harder didn't lead to school success, I stopped trying. Despite all the time and effort I invested, positive results were few and far between. The constant invalidation, misunderstandings, and shaming was just too much to bear. My best wasn't good enough. Dealing with this day in and day out—believing that it's all your fault and having no faith in yourself—is exhausting and leads to low self-esteem. I see this with my students time and again.

But, like me and the many people I've helped, you, too, can improve!

Fantasy Football

Parents need to understand how difficult participating in sports can be for their children. When I've explained this to parents, most are empathic and open to finding alternative activities in which their children could succeed.

> I once had a student who was terrified of participating in sports. But his father had been a football player and wanted more than anything to have his son play the sport. He insisted his son participate and refused to accept his limitations. He was embarrassed to have a son who couldn't play the game. He forced his son to practice relentlessly and shamed him for poor performance. We talked about having him take some art classes instead, as he was gifted in drawing, but his dad viewed this as both a cop-out and as an inappropriate hobby for a boy.
>
> The student's mother was a school psychologist and knew how damaging this was to her son. In addition to being bullied at school, he was also being bullied at home. Yet she could not stop her husband from his cruel behavior. This child became so anxious that he developed symptoms of OCD (obsessive compulsive disorder), such as repeatedly counting objects and washing his hands until they were raw. When people are under stress, the symptoms of dormant diagnoses increase. Eventually his mother prevailed, he dropped out of football, and his OCD symptoms greatly reduced.

Some kids refuse to participate in gym class when instructors are unaware or insensitive to their visual-spatial and motor difficulties. I was one of those kids who always had one reason or another why I couldn't participate:

I didn't feel well, had left my gym clothes at home, had a bad period, and anything else I could conjure up to get out of class.

Unlike adults, kids don't have the option to steer clear of sports activities. In most states, students have to pass gym all four high school years to graduate. Parents need to work it out with the school's Child Study Team to identify adaptive physical education alternatives or accommodations within the student's IEP.

My poor visual-spatial skills also made it difficult to find my locker in between classes, delaying me getting to my next class on time. I would often get lost in the building because the lockers looked the same to me. Plus, I had a hard time carrying my things while walking. I needed to go slowly to avoid dropping my things. Classroom and physical education teachers may not understand why navigating the halls or participating in sports is difficult because they do not have a diagnosis or the reason is not apparent to the naked eye. I spent a lot of time in detention for all the demerits I accumulated from being late.

Lost in Space

Getting lost, because of poor visual-spatial skills, is an all-too-familiar experience for many children and adults, even in familiar places. Offices, at work, schools, malls, and amusement parks can look very different depending on your vantage point. I once worked with a college student who got lost on campus grounds. He couldn't find his way back to the path that he had taken and had no idea how close he was to the nearest building, and his cell phone was dead. Security went looking for him after he was missing for quite some time. When found, he was so embarrassed by his close proximity to the path and the campus buildings.

It is typical for those with NVLD to struggle with spatial awareness—knowing where their body is in space in relation to objects, places, and other people. I cringe at the thought of how long this student would have been out there had no one noticed he was missing. He reported that he panicked and kept going around in circles, unable to find his way out. It's always a good idea to carry a compact cell phone charger with you to prevent yourself from getting in these types of situations.

You're Not College Material

Though I fully expected to go to college like the rest of my peers, my high school guidance counselor had little hope for me. He did not believe I was "college material" and had no qualms about telling me so. He was an authority figure and an educational professional whose job it was to guide me. If he didn't think I was worthy of success, then who was I to not believe him?

Granted, at that time, I *wasn't* college material, but that didn't mean I would never be. Like many others with NVLD, I needed more time to develop the skills to fulfill my potential. Had my guidance counselor been interested in helping me prepare for my future, I believe my outlook at that time would not have been so bleak. I often wonder what he would have said if he knew that I ultimately graduated college with honors, became a teacher, started my own learning center, and received many accolades for my work.

> ### Never Let Anyone Determine Who You Are and What You Can or Cannot Be!
> Teachers can contribute to and compound the damage to the psyche by dimming and even extinguishing a student's light. When teachers focus on their more promising students, neurodiverse students get lost in the mix. It hurt to watch my peers excitedly planning the next chapter in their lives, even though outwardly it appeared as if I couldn't have cared less.

People with learning difficulties have significantly contributed to society. We must stop labeling NDs as inferior because they do not perform according to the so-called standard of normality. What would have happened if Einstein or Edison, for example, had bought into their teachers' beliefs about them—that they were unteachable and wouldn't amount to much? One doesn't have to look far to see other accomplished individuals who have had similar experiences.

Thank goodness for Lynne, a childhood friend who insisted I go to college. Every time I gave her a reason why I couldn't go, she wouldn't accept it and continued to push me until I enrolled. I was twenty-two years old when I started college.

I had spent years thinking I was stupid, worthless, and lazy. I was so depressed I was barely able to function. My existence boiled down to sleeping, eating fast food, and going to school, with very little self-care and poor hygiene. In between classes, I lay down in my car, paralyzed by depression. I really wanted to work part-time, have friends, go to parties, and focus on my studies, but in reality, my lack of social skills and my academic struggles made it too difficult.

I had no idea how to study, manage my time, organize my work, or prepare for tests. I had been pushed through the public school system, and I wasn't prepared for the demands of college. I had to figure out how to compensate for this lack of skills. I had to work longer and harder than others to succeed. It took me an extra year to complete college, which is common for those with NVLD and other learning disabilities. Sometimes they may take even longer.

Looking for Answers

I did not know why I had such a hard time learning and functioning, which devastated me. I was so distraught that I decided I needed to know if I was mentally impaired. During college, I had a neuropsychological evaluation that showed that my intellect was average to above average.

I relentlessly questioned the psychologist how she could be so sure of that. When I asked her for my IQ score, she wouldn't give it to me. She explained that it didn't matter what the score was because I was doing college-level work at the honors level and was getting good grades, and I was gifted in writing. I concluded she was lying to me to not hurt my feelings. Can you imagine being so desperate and emotionally battered to actually think and believe you are mentally impaired in some way?

I am grateful the psychologist didn't disclose my IQ test scores because that would have traumatized me. Although NVLD was virtually unheard of at the time, she knew my test results were inaccurate. I shudder to think how things could have gone differently had I not seen a professional who was able to make sense of the discrepancy between my verbal and perceptual reasoning (visual-spatial) scores.

The psychologist assigned a graduate student who was studying to become a therapist to meet with me regularly. He was baffled by me and felt that in terms of social and emotional functioning, I was years behind my peers and more like a teenager. He didn't know how to help me.

I had to learn to catch up to my peers the hard way, with no training or support. I found myself in many situations that I had no idea how to handle, with some of them downright scary. Today, assistance is available for social skills training and social-emotional learning. It is critical to an NVLDer's well-being to understand they are not inferior. Having a brain-based disorder is just as legitimate as having diabetes or a heart murmur.

Years later, I discovered the work of the late Sue Thompson on NVLD and realized this was what I had. After a second assessment, I was told my scores were indicative of NVLD, but I could not receive a formal diagnosis because NVLD wasn't recognized in the *DSM*. Today, some professionals make the diagnosis even though it's still not yet officially recognized.

You're *Not* Your IQ Score!

Traditionally, IQ testing has not qualified as evidence of the need for accommodations, including extra time on tests, frequent breaks, and standardized testing spread out over multiple days. Unless the IQ testing conditions accommodate the needs of the individual test-taker, the scores may be inaccurate. Unfortunately, for those with learning disabilities, this isn't the way IQ tests are given. It takes an astute neuropsychologist, with a background in NVLD, to make an accurate diagnosis, as it's up to the evaluator to decide if the IQ scores are valid and representative of the person's ability.

Meet Jason

Jason's parents were at a loss as to how to help him. They had been to many professionals, with little success. The results of his psychological evaluation indicated that Jason didn't have the capacity to do his schoolwork because he was "mentally retarded." It recommended that Jason be taken out of public school because he could not be helped within a resource room and mainstream school setting.

There are two problems with this. First, by 2012, the term *retarded* was (and still is) considered derogatory and no longer used in neuropsychological reports. Second, it is illegal for a school to turn a student away, as all students with a disability have the right to free appropriate public education (FAPE), as guaranteed by the Rehabilitation Act of 1973 and the Individuals with Disabilities Education Act (IDEA).

Unbeknownst to his parents, Jason had overheard them discussing the results of his evaluation. Jason took the words "mental retardation" literally and interpreted them as the truth. He couldn't tell from his parents' tone of voice that they knew it wasn't true.

By the time I met him, Jason was beaten down and had given up. No matter how hard he tried at school, it didn't help. He already thought he was dumb and worthless, and after he had overheard his parents' conversation with the school, he was convinced he was retarded. After all, those were the words he heard, so it must be true.

Jason started talking about not wanting to live anymore, which unfortunately is common for some people with NVLD. I referred Jason's parents to an eye movement desensitization and reprocessing (EMDR) specialist to help him cope with the trauma he had experienced over the years. EMDR has been used successfully to treat those who have suffered from traumatic events.

My own conclusion, after I conducted an informal assessment, which is not the same as a psychological evaluation, was that Jason was on the autistic spectrum. I based my assessment on his mannerisms, eye contact, affect, and poor verbal and nonverbal communication skills. It never occurred to me that he might have NVLD since his verbal expressive skills were also in the lower ranges. Most individuals with NVLD score in the average to superior range for verbal language skills.

While the NVLD diagnosis explained his academic difficulties, it did not explain why Jason spoke so little at school. In my experience, it's unusual for someone with NVLD to be as nonresponsive as Jason. What I usually see is that the more the person doesn't understand, the more anxious they get, and the more they use their words and vocabulary to compensate.

It turned out that Jason's understanding of nonverbal communication was so limited that he was hesitant to respond. Fearing he would look foolish, he protected himself by being very careful in the way he spoke and the words he chose. This made him appear as functioning far below his intellectual level. It was as if his teachers were speaking a foreign language.

Over the weeks we worked together, as he began to trust me, Jason became quite a chatterbox! He was also able to do things with me that someone who was intellectually disabled would not be able to do. When he didn't understand what I was saying, he would ask me lots of questions to make up for the information he was missing. It was during this time that I began to wonder if he could have NVLD. I referred his parents to an experienced and reputable neuropsychologist who knew about NVLD. He concluded that Jason did have NVLD along with other learning disabilities.

Had Jason's parents followed the course of action the school had recommended, he would have been placed in a special school for those with intellectual disabilities. He would have been stigmatized, and his life would have taken a much different path. The work Jason did with me on cognitive skills training and social-emotional learning, along with EMDR and some other healing modalities, helped him to find success and enjoy life. He was able to go back to a new public high school, attend mainstream classes taught on his grade level, and make friends. As I write, Jason is doing well in college!

The Importance of Accommodations

I needed to pass a noncredit course in math to be able to take the required college-level math courses. I failed the final exam, but because my score was on the border of passing, I was eligible to participate in a weeklong review class during Christmas break and then retake the exam. I finally passed, but I still had two more classes to take to meet the math requirements to graduate college.

Had I had accommodations in college, I would have obtained the math grades of which I was capable. Accommodations provide extra support that enables students with learning disabilities to meet their potential. According to the Learning Disabilities Association of America, students must advocate for accommodations in college by working with personnel in the Disability Services office. (Every college that receives federal funding is required to offer Disability Services.) They determine if students' requests are supported by the documentation each student has to provide. To receive accommodations, students must also be evaluated and diagnosed with a learning disability by an educational or neuropsychologist.

Example of a Math Accommodation

Visual presentations need to be altered for those with NVLD to help compensate for their weaknesses and assist them to perform tasks. In math, for example, some students are unable to process the visual elements of assignments from textbooks or handouts. One way for teachers to accommodate this issue is to create a separate sheet of paper with boxes for each math problem, which allows students to process the math problem better visually. Such accommodations help students learn better and demonstrate their true abilities.

Students who have an IEP can ask for math accommodations to be included in the plan. However, it's not uncommon for schools to fail to provide these services. As a former special education teacher, I have repeatedly advocated for my students in their mainstream classes to get those teachers to comply with the students' IEPs. Unfortunately, some professionals see accommodations as providing the student with an advantage over their peers.

This is like saying students who wear glasses (an accommodation) have an unfair edge over others who don't. Nothing could be further from the truth. A teacher wouldn't even think about having students remove their glasses, nor would they get away with it if they did. Wearing glasses simply removes the learning obstacles faced by the student due to poor eyesight. The same is true of accommodations for those with learning disabilities, as they make it possible for them to learn like everyone else.

Your child is entitled to these services, so be the squeaky wheel that gets the grease! Keep in mind that providing accommodations and modifications, as well as study skills, is much more effective after the remediation of poor executive function / cognitive skills, ideally in elementary school. Students need a higher level of motivation and intact processing skills to effectively implement executive functioning and cognitive skills. Typically, by the time they are introduced in middle school to high school, students have little interest in using them, as they are weary from their ongoing struggles.

Modifications versus Accommodations

Although modifications are different from accommodations, the two are often confused. According to Understood, an organization representing unconventional learners, accommodations can help students learn the same material as their peers. This allows them to meet the same expectations. Modifications help students who are far behind their peers to master course content by changing the curriculum to better meet their needs.

While modifications can be provided during the primary, middle, and secondary school years, they are not provided at the college level because college students are held to uniform expectations. Accommodations do not change academic standards, so you can receive them in college.

How I Graduated College with Honors: My Workarounds

Since I was not classified as learning disabled, I wasn't aware I would have been eligible to receive accommodations, and I had to find my own way through college. When I cook, I often swap out ingredients I do not like in my favorite recipes and replace them with alternatives that suit my tastes. I took this approach to college and developed my own strategies to cope with my learning challenges. I know that no one tactic works for everyone. Can you use your successes as a platform to create your own system? I used the strategies described below in combination with standard methods to graduate college with honors.

Find the Best Instructors for Your Learning Style

The instructor can make or break your success. I made it my business to ask other students about the instructors they had had in the classes I needed to take. It was crucial for me to have professors who were passionate about their subject and skilled in their delivery of course content and materials. Ask about the instructor's grading methods: do they give pop quizzes, base tests on class notes or textbooks, expect frequent participation in class, and assign group projects?

Most important, try to determine if the instructor is open to students with learning disabilities and understands their needs for accommodations. Anna, one of my college student clients with NVLD and ADHD, was entitled to accommodations, but her professor didn't make it easy on her. During class one day, he made a snide remark about how some students are privileged and have an unfair advantage over other students by getting untimed tests. She found another professor with a different mindset and actually enjoyed the class.

Pacing Yourself

Instead of taking five classes a semester, like most of my peers, I took four to reduce stress and to give me the extra time I needed to focus and determine my own pace. I also took one course each summer. When I had courses that were difficult for me (except math), I took them along with less demanding electives to allow me to better focus on the more strenuous classes.

My biggest fear was being unable to pass the math courses required to get my college degree. What worked for me was to take approximately 80 percent of my classes and leave the math requirements until the end. That way, I did not get discouraged early on in my studies. Having everything completed before tackling math gave me the momentum to cross the finish line.

Grade Point Average (GPA) and the Pass/Fail Option

It was important to me to have a high GPA. To do this, I took the pass/fail option for my math classes whenever I could. Instead of getting a grade for the class, you pass the course with a grade of D or higher without affecting your GPA. However, if you don't pass, your GPA will be affected by having a zero added to it. Be sure to check with your college or university because some require a C or higher to pass, and if you do fail, it may be handled differently. The pass/fail option may not be available for all classes depending on the college you attend.

Dropping Classes

The add/drop process allows you to withdraw after the class starts as long as you meet the cutoff date. This gave me enough time to see how I was doing in the class. If I was heading toward failure, I would withdraw. It wouldn't count toward my GPA and appeared as a W, for withdrawal, on my transcript. I did this in earth science and a math class when the instructor wasn't a good fit for me.

Early-Morning Classes

I had a terrible time getting up, and I hated taking early-morning classes. People with ADHD often have interrupted sleep patterns, and it takes longer for their brains to wake up. NVLDers and NDs have a higher rate of depression, which also makes getting up and out of bed difficult.

To work around this, I enrolled in as few morning classes as possible, but there were classes I needed that were only offered in the early mornings. After hitting the snooze button for the last time, I would rush around like a maniac, trying to get ready to get to class on time, which did not always work. I tried different tactics and kept trying different things until I found stress-free ways that worked. Medication helps some people with ADHD, but not all, and I needed to find a substitute.

The caffeine in coffee worked to get me out of bed. To get to 8:00 a.m. classes, I set my alarm for 6:00 a.m. and immediately guzzled a bottle of caffeinated iced tea that I had put next to my bed the previous evening. I took my shower the night before—get ready for this; it's a doozy—and slept in the clothes I would wear the next day. I know, crazy, right? I wore a clean T-shirt and leggings to bed. In the morning, I'd put on my socks and sneakers and a headband. Finally, I would grab my book bag and energy bar and head off to class looking like I had just come from the gym!

VAKT

VAKT (visual, auditory, kinesthetic, tactile) is a multisensory teaching method based on the belief that students learn best when information is presented in different modalities. Kinesthetic is moving while learning; tactile is hands-on learning, including writing. I learned about VAKT in one of my special education college classes and used it to improve my learning process. It helped to strengthen brain connections and form new neural pathways. This made learning academic material easier and faster and improved my long-term memory. Here are some of the tools I created using VAKT principles.

- *Reading*

  It was hard for me to focus while sitting still to complete my reading assignments. I recorded myself reading and listened while exercising or walking to comprehend the material.

- *Notes from Reading Assignments*

  I would take notes from the recordings of my reading assignments to summarize concepts. If I needed to, I'd take it one step further and type these notes, which helped me to study from them.

- *Notes from Class Lectures*

  If I was lucky, I found other students willing to let me photocopy their notes. I'd explain to them that I had difficulty writing quickly, so I would miss important information. I read, recorded, and typed them, or just highlighted them, depending on what I needed for understanding the material.

- *Note-Taking*

  Even if I had someone else's notes, I still took my own. I created blank outline forms to use during class lectures. Filling in the blanks helped me to structure and organize topics with supporting details. Otherwise, I'd try to write down everything the instructor said, and I'd wind up with a bunch of notes looking like "chicken scratch."

- *Recording Class Lectures*

  Some instructors allowed me to record class lectures. Find out if there is a schoolwide policy or if it is up to the individual instructors. If possible include in your accommodations plan.

- *Mantras*

  I can't tell you how many times I wanted to give up, especially when I was coping with depression and anxiety. I developed mantras that I'd say to myself over and over and over: "No matter what you do, time will still pass. You will still be twenty-seven whether you stay in college or not." This meant that I might as well stay in college and be twenty-seven with a college degree. Create your own mantra to combat your thoughts when you're discouraged.

- *Vision Boards*

  I created vision boards to help me stay on track—to keep my eye on the prize. I looked for images in magazines that inspired me, cut them out, and pasted them on poster boards. I had one board by my desk and another in my bedroom, places where I would see them many times throughout the day. I still make vision boards to inspire me and to meet goals.

- *Seeing in Your Mind's Eye*

    Do you remember seeing some students look up while taking a test? I had a teacher who would say to those of us who were doing this, "What are you doing looking up? Are the answers on the ceiling?" What I didn't know at the time was that we were looking into our "mind's eye" and seeing a page in a textbook or in our notes that had the information to answer some of the questions on the test.

    When you look up, especially to the left, you are subconsciously using the occipital lobe of your brain, where visual information is stored. Right now, look up to the left and picture your bedroom in your mind's eye. Can you see your bed, furniture, the color of your walls? Most people can do this, but some with NVLD cannot. If not, you can practice and improve your visual processing by visualizing places or objects in your mind's eye. If there is information on a chart or in your notes that you know will be on a test, spend some time looking at it, put it away, look up to the ceiling, and practice seeing it in your mind's eye.

- *Songs*

    How many times have you heard songs from years ago and still knew all the words? We retain the words because we heard them repeatedly. Essentially, our auditory and memory systems have programmed the songs into our brains. This is why you can remember the words to a song when you were a kid but can't remember what you learned in class as easily and effortlessly. Advertisers use jingles to sell products because they are powerful marketing tools. I often picked songs that I liked and wrote new lyrics using the information I needed to learn.

College Isn't the Only Way

College isn't the only path to success. The concept of hiring for skills rather than degrees has gained steam in recent years, and employers are beginning to take notice. There is a shortage of tradespeople nowadays, and as the older generation retires, tradespeople will be even more in demand. Plus, it's not uncommon for tradespeople to earn more than college graduates. While trades rely heavily on visual-spatial and executive functioning skills, some NVLDers have success in these fields. And, finally, a college degree doesn't necessarily guarantee employment success.

If you do decide to go to college, some of the lessons I learned may also help you to succeed. You don't need to do all these things for each class. I'm simply sharing with you some of the things that helped me. Take what you like, and leave the rest.

Lessons Learned
Know What You Want and Need
Knowing what I wanted to do with my life and what to study in school played a huge role in giving me the courage and motivation to reach my goals. My passion was to help kids who struggled in school. I didn't want anyone to go through what I did. Had I not known what I wanted, I wouldn't have been as driven! It's important to find what holds your interest to have the focus and drive to succeed. You have to love what you study to weather the challenges of college-level academics.

I also wasn't mature enough socially or emotionally to attend college right after high school or at a school away from home. I needed time to further develop and didn't enroll until I was twenty-two years old. If this is you or your child, you can postpone college and find a job while you work on improving your social skills and identifying your passion and educational goals.

Find Inspiration
Identify a role model whose success you'd like to emulate. When I was feeling defeated, I would find inspiration in the lives of others who overcame their struggles. I'd tell myself if they could do it, so could I. Of my many role models, Thomas Edison was the most inspiring. What really got me was how many times he failed (over ten thousand) when working to create the lightbulb.

He continued to try another way repeatedly, viewed his unsuccessful attempts as learning, and by process of elimination, got to his goal. Thomas Edison said it best "Never get discouraged if you fail. Learn from it. Keep trying."

Also, watching the biographical movie *Rudy* made a huge impact on me. In this extraordinary movie, you will see how Rudy persevered by refusing to give up.

Be Your Own GPS

NVLDers can be all-or-nothing thinkers—they tend to get the details but not the big picture. Do not let this prevent you from realizing your potential! Remember that to keep on top of your game, you need to constantly challenge your right-or-wrong, black-or-white thinking.

If you are frustrated in your efforts, be your own GPS and try another route. There are many ways to arrive at a destination: on the fastest route, the shortest route, a route with no tolls, a route with rest stops along the way. If you take a wrong turn, your GPS will automatically adjust the directions to keep you on track. It will also take you another way if there are obstacles on a route. You will ultimately arrive at your destination, just not necessarily by the original route.

Keep your eye on the prize, and try different ways. You may have to reevaluate and modify your goals, like my student who wanted to become a nurse and instead became a medical assistant (see chapter 5).

Ask for Help

I couldn't receive accommodations because I didn't have a diagnosis. In fact, I had no idea I was learning disabled and had NVLD. I just knew something was off and accepted that I was one of those students who had to work harder than others. Even so, I was able to use tutoring services on campus at no charge. I often see students who do not make use of the academic support services available to them. Many drop out of college, which might have been prevented had they taken advantage of the academic and emotional support service available to them.

There are also many tools available to help you, such as tutoring, apps, voice-to-text software programs, planners, and study buddies. Don't be afraid to ask for help or to use the support services available to you.

Keep an Open Mind

Think about the challenges you have faced. What changes did you make to overcome your difficulties? Look for clues as to how you achieved success. Remember, it is not about right or wrong but what works for you!

Chapter 5

Finding the Right Job

Most NVLDers and NDs (neurodiverse people) find their own way in the neurotypical world by pushing beyond the limits, developing a strong work ethic and problem-solving in unconventional ways. These traits benefit all areas of their lives, including careers. Jobs that are predictable and structured seem to be the best fit for NVLDers. Jobs that are too structured and menial in nature tend to be unsatisfying for those who have a love of learning.

In this chapter, I have included examples of my own and others' employment challenges and successes to highlight workplace issues faced by those with NVLD that reflect their unique skills. It is my hope that these stories will help you realize your potential and find the job that is right for you. Check out "Employment Inspiration" at the end of this chapter.

Fast-Food Frenzy

My work challenges started at my very first job in high school at a local Burger King. Fast-food restaurants are, of course, fast-paced, and my poor executive functioning skills prevented me from meeting the simultaneous demands of the job.

In my haste to fill orders, I had trouble paying attention to details. For instance, because at a glance tartar sauce and mayo looked the same to me, customers got fish filets with mayo and burgers with tartar. Looking back, if I were able to put labels on the containers, I would have solved that problem. I could not transition easily from one task to the next, like most of my coworkers could. I coped by hovering over the soda machine and filling all of the drink orders each server placed. It was easier to manage more requests for the same menu item than switch from soda to burgers to fries and back again.

The thought that I might, at a moment's notice, be stationed at the drive-through window and have to handle money caused me to panic. I took frequent bathroom breaks to gather myself. I also escaped from the kitchen by going into the dining area to clear the trash and clean the tables, a task I could handle independently while also avoiding my peers.

Next, I was hired by a local pizzeria that did not provide job training. I was expected to learn my role by watching other employees. That meant learning from visual observation, which is very challenging for someone with NVLD. It's imperative for people with NVLD to also be given verbal instructions to master tasks. The owner and staff spoke Italian, so it wasn't always easy to understand them. The cooks had devised their own communication system to indicate to servers when food was ready by clapping their hands a specific number of times for each item. One clap meant a pizza was ready, two claps were for sandwiches, three for salads, and four for entrées.

I again found something I could better do to draw attention away from my difficulties: positioning myself next to the phone and taking incoming orders. I was expected to answer the phone by saying "Pizza Palace," the name of the pizzeria, but I thought other workers were saying, "Pizza Place," when they answered the phone. Poor auditory processing is common for people with learning difficulties who struggle to filter spoken language from background noise.

One day, the owner overheard me answering the phone with "Pizza Place." He pulled me aside and said the job wasn't working out for me and then gave me a generous amount of cash. I walked home, crying the whole way, not knowing what was wrong with me. I just wanted to be like other kids my age and be able to do the things the other kids did. I thought I was stupid. I didn't yet know or understand that I was neurodivergent.

Educational Gaps on the Job

When I was twenty, I worked at a transportation company where the consequences of my gaps in learning caught up with me. I answered calls to arrange for package pickups and deliveries. The company didn't deliver outside of the United States. One day, a man wanted to ship a package to New Mexico. I told him that we didn't ship outside the United States and therefore couldn't deliver the package to New Mexico. Word got around the office, and I was the talk of the town.

I can only imagine what you, the reader, are thinking now! I actually thought twice about putting this in the book, but I want you to be aware of this conundrum to prevent similar situations for you or your child.

Why didn't I know something so basic? As I described in the chapter on school, I had missed a lot of important content. My focusing difficulties and trouble visually discerning the states on a map were the cause of this particular mistake. It was easier to act like I didn't care than to look foolish in front of my classmates. Consequently, I never processed that information, and it never made it to my long-term memory.

None of these jobs provided me enough income to support myself or enough challenge to meet my potential. The worst jobs for those with learning disabilities are those where the tasks exacerbate their struggles. Not being able to perform these tasks has nothing to do with one's ability, although it appears that way to others, leaving NVLDers exposed to bullying on the job. NVLDers tend to shine in jobs with a high level of autonomy, flexibility, intellectual stimulation, and outside-the-box thinking. It is all about finding the right fit.

Following My Dream

As you know by now, my experiences made me determined to help others like me. I became a special education teacher, and I excelled at what I did because of my background. Since I had many of the same experiences, I truly understood my students, could relate to them on a personal level, and was able to help them navigate the school experience and enhance their ability to learn. I received an award from the governor of New Jersey for the work I did to develop educational methods and materials that made a positive difference in learning for my students.

I left teaching, after receiving tenure, for several reasons. One day, I was in my car with another teacher on our way to lunch. It started to rain. My poor visual-motor skills can make using mechanical items difficult. My coworker, another special education teacher, saw me struggling with the windshield wipers and belittled me by saying, "How can you not know how to turn on the windshield wipers in your own car?" I should have explained to her that, like some of our students, I have visual-motor integration difficulties. I didn't do it because I was humiliated, and feelings of inadequacy flooded my mind.

I began to question the system. Working in an environment where I had to navigate the structures of institutional and social systems that didn't understand me and my students took a toll on me. I wanted to make a difference in the lives of the students, and I felt that I couldn't have the impact I wanted within the educational system.

My students had difficulty socially interacting with each other, and I spent most of the school day on behavior modification and building self-esteem. It became necessary to teach them social skills before they could learn academics. At that time, social-emotional learning wasn't a part of the curriculum so I had to create my own program.

Their IEP plans and traditional interventions weren't enough to catch them up to the grade level of their peers. I grew frustrated and wanted to provide better long-term solutions that I couldn't offer in the public school system. I needed to find another way.

So, I chose a different path to fulfill my dream and better use my energy and talents to help others, like me, change the course of their lives and reach their full potential.

Making It on My Own: Becoming an Entrepreneur

I began researching the science behind learning to get to the root of learning problems instead of going around them. When I finally found what I was looking for, I wanted to start my own consulting business. Once again, my dad was there for me and instrumental in helping me to take the risk. He and others in our family had started their own businesses. Although my husband was concerned, my father reassured him by saying, "Let her go; she'll be fine. This is how we do things in our family." Like other immigrants, they were entrepreneurs long before the term became fashionable because they had to find a way to feed their families.

When there was no way, they made their own way.

It's common for neurodiverse individuals to find different ways of doing things. Having a different way of thinking pushes past the limits of traditional models, breaking molds and creating new paradigms. This also puts them in a unique position to see future needs and trends.

I opened my business in 1997, and the response was amazing. There were no places that provided executive functioning development (processing skills) and social skills programs along with the other services I offered. I was inundated with families looking for help. Parents traveled for miles to enroll their children of all ages and watched them begin to realize their potential. They were getting better grades, their behavior improved, and they were happier at home and school. They learned to complete schoolwork independently and to make and keep friends. Best of all, they demonstrated improved self-esteem and confidence and a real eagerness to learn!

Keys may unlock doors, but you can build your own doors and make your own keys!

Entrepreneurship essentially is creating your own position and job description as opposed to working for others. If you're ready to skip this section because you think it's impossible, bear with me here. NVLDers and NDs think and do things differently; when they are emotionally ready to embrace their differences and willing to work on themselves, then they begin to bloom. Like the aftermath of a hurricane, people begin to rise above, survey the damage, and start the process of rebuilding.

However, no one can give you that determination, do the work for you, or push you. You must want it *so* badly

you would do anything for it. Once you feel that, you will be unstoppable.

Lynne's encouragement enabled me to enroll in college. My dad's belief in me led me to start my own business. He thought the best way for me to succeed was to define success on my own terms. Neither of them did the work for me, but they were there to support me. In another chapter, I'll outline how to determine what support you need and where to find it.

Working for Yourself

You may think you can't work for yourself, but it may be one of the best options you have. Yes, there will be challenges to overcome, but that's also true of working for someone else. You can do things on your terms and have the control you need without worrying about how you will fit in and meet the demands of a boss. Instead of waiting for others to approve of your work or promote you, it's possible you may be able to do this yourself by working for yourself. One of the great things about working for yourself is that you can design your job and give yourself your own accommodations.

Patching

Depending on one's level of skill, education, and emotional state, finding a way to make an income can be done with patching. Essentially patching is working a couple of jobs or combining a job with a side gig to make ends meet.

Chloe loved working with toddlers, but it wasn't enough money for her to support herself. She rented a small space and started "Mommy and Me" classes. Stay-at-home moms would bring their children to a themed arts and crafts class based on a children's book. Chloe involved the children in an interactive story with props and costumes during story time. While the children were playing, the moms would enjoy some much-needed social time with each other. The children made a craft related to the story, followed by "snack time" with their moms. She had a full schedule every weekday.

Chloe "patched" this along with a part-time job and a steady schedule of dog-sitting in people's homes while they were away on vacations. This worked out well for her, as she was still covered by her parents' insurance, which gave her some time to figure out what she would do in the future when she would have to pay for her own health insurance. Chloe needed the time to mature socially and emotionally. Eventually, she enrolled in school to become a medical technician and landed a full-time job with health benefits after she graduated. She also continued dog-sitting to make some extra money. Chloe was able to find success by patching and creating the work she loved.

Working for Others

The challenges that are unique to those with NVLD can be both strengths and weaknesses in the workplace. For someone with NVLD, getting the job is often easier than keeping it. NVLDers who have insight into their difficulties can actually razzle and dazzle prospective employers during the interview process with their exceptional verbal expressive skills.

The most successful individuals are those who channel their fear, anxiety, and energy toward researching how to master the interview process. Much like cramming for an exam, they'll give their undivided attention, called "hyperfocusing," to preparing for the interview, as well as doing extensive research to learn about the history of the company. Many create and memorize their own scripts to answer standard questions, like "Tell me about yourself" and "What are your strengths and weaknesses?" Mentally placing themselves in the interview, rehearsing in front of a mirror, and recording mock interviews can clench the job. If you are not already doing these things, they will greatly improve your interview performance.

Keeping the job is another story. This requires responding to situations and tasks on the spot. You can't prepare ahead for all the interactions that happen each day. Most neurotypicals don't need to diligently think about how they are coming across to others by monitoring their body language and reading others because that's already a subconscious process that happens automatically.

NVLDers do need to be cognizant of how others perceive them. Most NVLDers start out at the bottom rung of the ladder, like most NTs do at the beginning of their careers, but they need to spend more time there while they gradually gain the skills to advance to higher-level positions.

This is to be expected as they go through a variety of jobs learning through their experiences and the process of going up the ladder, down, up, and down until they are able to compensate for their executive functioning deficits and refine their communication skills.

Know Thyself

The key to finding the right job/career fit is self-awareness—knowing what you do best, the challenges you face, and your pitfalls. Mental health and emotional well-being also factor into what is suitable employment. Research the responsibilities and tasks of the jobs, and consider these factors:

- technical skills—what you like to do and what you are good at
- education—the knowledge and the ability to accomplish the specific tasks of the job
- social skills—the ability to fit in with others

For example, if you find that dealing with lots of different personalities is exhausting and requires more time and focus than what you put into your work, look for jobs in companies with a small staff and in fields where individuality and creativity are valued.

I highly recommend, if you have not done so already, to get a neuropsychological evaluation from a professional who understands NVLD. If you cannot afford a neuropsychological assessment, check with your state's vocational rehabilitation agency, as you most likely will be eligible to receive one at no cost to you. If you are able to get a diagnosis, even if it's not NVLD, it will help you gain the information you need about yourself to assist you in finding the right fit in the workforce. This may include college, vocational training, working your way up at a current or future position, learning from a mentor, using your area of interest/expertise in employable positions, or working for yourself.

That said, I advise finding an independent career counselor or someone else outside of the agency that provided the assessment to interpret your results in regard to suitable employment. Some of my clients have been given very limited options for employment through state agencies when they were capable of higher-level, more fulfilling positions and earning more income. If you decide to work with a career counselor, it's imperative you obtain the services of one who has experience working with the learning-disabled population and who will take the time to learn about NVLD. Locating such a professional can be difficult because most are not trained in this area and may do more harm than good.

Mapping Careers with LD and ADD Clients: Guidebook and Case Studies by Raise Abby Janus is a must-read. A former director of assessment and counseling at the Personnel Sciences Center in New York City and an adjunct instructor in the School for Continuing Education of New York University, Janus covers the misperceptions of career counselors and employers who tag those with learning disabilities and

ADHD as difficult and lazy because of their "invisible" differences and social behaviors. You'll learn about the therapeutic approach to career assessment, how to find the right job fit and improve job performance, practical solutions to avoid problems before they occur, and more. Do yourself a favor and get a copy. You can find used copies on eBay and Amazon.

Some people with NVLD are unable to work because of their circumstances, while others may be able to find sufficient work but not make enough money to support themselves. Applying for financial assistance may be necessary in both of these scenarios. I do not recommend this until you have explored every avenue, as you may be underestimating yourself or your child. Treatment for learned helplessness and social and executive functioning skills; medical care for depression and anxiety, which may or may not include medication management under your doctor's supervision; vocational training; and other interventions can lead to better employment outcomes.

After exhausting all of your options, you can then make a better decision as to whether or not to apply for social/disability benefits through your state. If this is the case, you may be able to find a lawyer who will take on the case and be paid once you are awarded benefits. You may have to make several applications to the state before it is approved. In the meantime, call your township's housing department to find out what financial resources are available to you in your community. You may be able to access low-income housing the town has developed that is not a part of the federal Section 8 program.

Company Culture

Understanding the culture of a company will help you determine if it would be a good match for you. A positive workplace culture improves teamwork, raises morale, increases productivity and efficiency, and enhances retention of the workforce. Job satisfaction, collaboration, and work performance are all enhanced. Most important, a positive work environment reduces stress in employees.

Some companies are more formal. They may have a dress code as well as strict expectations and methods for how things are done. Some provide more autonomy and are not as concerned about how the job is done as long as the end result is quality work. They may allow for more individuality and creativity and have a casual dress code.

Do your research. Look at the ratings on www.glassdoor.com and other sites to read the opinions of former employees. The more you read, the more you will get a feel for the vibe of the company. If you can, contact some of the reviewers personally to see if they will answer questions about the company. Try to determine if the company is inclusive and values neurodiversity. Do they have any complaints filed against them? What is their mission statement? Do they have programs to help those in the community?

- *Number of Employees*

Company size can be an advantage or disadvantage depending on the position, tasks, and culture. Smaller companies usually run at a slower pace and offer more flexibility and can be more supportive. You may have more freedom to do things differently, such as implementing new ideas and wearing clothes more to your taste, thanks to a flexible dress code. Larger companies usually have more benefits, such as reimbursement for college tuition, better health plans, more vacation time, and other perks. However, you may need to interact with more people and adhere to more rules, which may cause you more stress.

- *To Tell or Not to Tell?*

Title I of the Americans with Disabilities Act (ADA) prohibits discrimination in employment and requires employers (with fifteen or more employees) to provide reasonable accommodations for employees with disabilities. However, whether or not you reveal your disability is a personal decision, and there are pros and cons to each choice. It is important to know the law and know the company's policy on hiring individuals with learning disabilities (see ldeamerica.org or www.ada.gov).

Many NDs choose to hide their difficulties and try to pass as neurotypical, fearing that disclosing will put their job at risk. There is conflicting advice among professionals about disclosure. I can't tell you what to do or what is the right answer for you without knowing your background, strengths, and weaknesses. The Learning Disabilities Association of America states that adults with learning disabilities find it best to disclose information only if accommodations will be required in a particular job.

I can only speak from my own experience and from working with others. The best outcomes have been in situations where my clients did not disclose during the interview. If you choose to disclose after you have accepted a position, you can either go to human resources and disclose to get accommodations, or you can start work and see how well you can manage on your own first by using your own strategies.

Be very careful, as timing is everything at this juncture. Make sure your work during this period is up to par and meeting the demands of the job as expected. If you are struggling, it's important that you disclose your learning disabilities to human resources before your superior documents your work as unsatisfactory. Most companies give you time to get acclimated and adjust your efforts before you are evaluated. Each company is different so be sure to find out what your current employer's policy is. You have set yourself up for the best scenario possible and have nothing to lose. Other professionals may disagree, but this is the stance I take based on years of experience both personally and professionally with NVLD.

It's not unheard of for companies to be mandated to hire a certain percentage of learning-disabled employees to meet antidiscrimination requirements, thus helping some to get their foot in the door. This is how Susan was able to obtain a job. When she asked for accommodations, her boss had no understanding of learning disabilities and thought this was an excuse, that she had no work ethic, and that she didn't want to work to meet her responsibilities. Unfortunately, at this company, after human resources met their quota, they had no interest in ensuring that the employees were doing OK or in training staff on how to work together. Susan could have hired an attorney, but she didn't have the resources to do this. She decided to file a complaint through human resources. When it became apparent that she wasn't getting anywhere, she chose to leave the company.

Some companies, however, provide training on learning disabilities and accommodations to department heads and follow up with employees to see how they are doing.

If you decide to disclose, it is important to know how your learning issues may impact your ability to do the job. Accommodations allow NDs to be productive, perform optimally on the job, and level the playing field between you and your NT coworkers. Knowing your strengths and weaknesses in relation to a particular job and knowing what accommodations you need will help you achieve success. These may include working in a quiet location away from others, wearing earbuds to listen to music (helps some to stay calm), using a white noise machine to filter out distractions, having extended time to meet deadlines, frequently meeting with a supervisor to stay on track, and starting or ending the workday at a different time.

Each company may have its own requirements and protocols for obtaining accommodations. Some companies may require a current neuropsychological evaluation proving that you have a learning disability. Such evaluations will include the specific supports (accommodations) you need to perform job-related tasks. If you are required to have a neuropsychological evaluation to receive accommodations, you may be able to get around this by submitting a letter from your doctor or therapist that states your diagnosis and the accommodations you need. Therapists are more apt to help you if you provide them the information needed by doing some of the legwork for them. Look online for examples of work accommodations, pick the ones that apply to you, and draft the letter with this list for your doctor or therapist. This may be sufficient to get what you need on the job. As mentioned, check with your state's vocational rehabilitation agency to obtain a neuropsychological assessment if it is required to receive accommodations on the job and you cannot afford to pay for the assessment yourself.

Small companies owned by an entrepreneur who likes and understands you can be great places to work. You may only need a conversation about how you work best, without revealing a diagnosis, to get the support that will help you perform optimally instead of providing a neuropsychological evaluation. For example, you might say, "I work best with structure and in a quiet area."

Meet Tom

Tom had a terrible concept of time and space. He also had trouble falling asleep at night, despite taking his last dose of medication for ADHD in the early afternoon. In addition, he had sleep apnea, and despite using a CPAP machine, he didn't get the amount or quality of sleep he needed. Not surprisingly, he had a horrible time waking up in the morning.

Many people with ADHD have a difficult time getting out of bed in the morning. Once they are physically up, it takes a few hours for the brain to mentally wake up and become functioning. Tom would force himself to get up on time and would be ready early only to get distracted before it was time to leave.

Tom excelled at his job, troubleshooting computer problems. He was able to zone in and stay focused to get the job done efficiently. The problem was the company was located on a large campus with many different buildings and departments. Each day, he used a golf cart to go to the buildings needing tech support. Every day, the route was different, and Tom would get lost because of his poor visual-spatial skills. He had trouble finding the correct pathways and going from one location to the next.

Because he was an asset to the company, it was to their advantage to work with him. They let him start an hour later in the morning, they added signs with arrows

> pointing the way to each named building, and when he needed verbal guidance, his boss gave him directions on the walkie-talkies. Helping Tom to get to the buildings on time meant more jobs were completed, which saved the company money and supported Tom's well-being.

Employment Inspiration

- ***Problem-Solving Patricia (Strength: Finding Alternative Solutions)***

Patricia worked at a well-known nonprofit organization. She was responsible for securing substantial donations from current and prospective donors. Patricia had had many setbacks in her personal and professional life and, as a result, learned how to problem-solve to meet her goals by thinking outside the box and finding alternative tactics. Her experiences and educational background gave her a strong sense of her capabilities.

Patricia's success with donors was remarkable. The company was so impressed with her performance and the process she developed that she was asked to create new modules based on her techniques and train others in the company on how to obtain similar results. Patricia had challenges on the job. She could come across as tactless at times. But, because she was an excellent employee, got results, and stood out from others, she was respected for the work she did. Although others saw her as quirky or different, her social skills didn't interfere with her success on the job. Her work performance compensated for her poor social skills.

- ***Self-Employed Sam (Difficulty with Social Skills)***
Self-employment works well for those who find that they consistently struggle with social interactions. For these people, it's a full-time job just to play detective and decipher nonverbal communication. This often hinders their ability to be team players and meet social expectations. When this takes precedence and the actual tasks of the job become secondary, it's time to move on to something else. Self-employed Sams are more likely to be satisfied and successful when using their intellectual skills.

The freedom of working for themselves can be liberating. They don't have to worry if they say or do something others misconstrue as offensive or if their need to ask excessive questions demonstrates a lack of intelligence. Self-employment enables them to "engineer" an environment tailored to their needs by relieving themselves of the burden and anxiety of "social politics," which may limit or block their success.

There are, however, positions with companies that simulate self-employment by offering options, such as working from home, flextime (flexible hours and schedules that allow you to vary workday start and finish times), and floating or flexible deadlines so you can work at your own pace. These conditions may reduce the amount of in-person communication with superiors and coworkers and mitigate the struggle with social issues. Without the stress of interpreting and navigating social interactions, anxiety is automatically decreased, allowing one to focus completely on the actual tasks of the job.

- ***Jobless Joe (Poor Executive Functioning, Time Management, Emotional Regulation, and Organizational Skills and Sleep Disturbances)***

Joe had chronic difficulties maintaining jobs for the long haul. No matter where he worked, his troubles seemed to follow him. Joe had gone through so many jobs the person who did his yearly taxes said he had never had anyone with so many W-2 forms. It wasn't until he started a job doing maintenance for a pool company that he was able to find success.

Setting his own schedule was a game-changer for Joe. Like Tom and me, Joe felt that getting up in the morning was equivalent to climbing Mt. Everest. Joe finally had the ability to set up his own appointments and work during the hours that were compatible with his brain. This job also afforded him the opportunity to utilize his creativity and social media skills, enabling him to add more value for his customers with new ideas, such as themed pool party packages. Joe was able to make more money from the commissions he earned by bringing in new clients. Eventually, he started his own pool maintenance company.

Joe also got the help he needed. To compensate for his poor executive functioning skills, I worked with him to customize and set up turn-key systems for his business. Hiring a bookkeeper kept him in check with his finances. Whether it's setting up a business or finding success as an employee, most NVLDers will need support to become self-sufficient and financially independent adults. Once they learn the skills and find the right support, they will gradually be able to manage on their own. Joe found his niche; he defined success on his own terms!

- ***Bullied Bill (Poor Reading and Writing Skills, Peer Pressure)***

Stories about bullying in the workplace break my heart. Although Bill had exceptional verbal intelligence and was a good conversationalist, his poor writing skills and dyslexia held him back from obtaining successful employment that matched his intellect. His job applications were full of misspelled words. The only jobs he could get were entry-level positions that required very few qualifications.

At thirty-two years old, Bill was working in the kitchen of a local establishment with a mix of high school and college kids. They saw him as a loser because he was working at a lower-level job in comparison to his age. Since he was unable to process tone of voice, he was unaware of when he was being mistreated. When he didn't react to their innuendos, they used explicit language to humiliate him.

At one point, when Bill was employed in a ravioli factory, where he only made minimum wage, two of his coworkers who were well-known bullies cornered him and roughed him up. When Bill started work at a printing company, he found that he really enjoyed it and excelled. In fact, he was recognized for his work and promoted. But the bullying did not stop. One of his coworkers who had a black belt in karate threatened him because he thought he deserved Bill's promotion.

Bill's parents expected him to contribute to the family as an adult living at home while having no idea of his NVLD and the seriousness of this disorder. They wanted to help their son but were tired of the drama of the never-ending fiascos he seemed to get into, essentially blaming him for his wayward ways. His parents didn't realize that he was easily manipulated. He became bitter, defensive, and rebellious and began to self-medicate with drugs and alcohol.

Having no way to support himself and hoping to straighten himself out, he enlisted in the navy, but the bullying continued from his peers and sometimes even his superiors. When he left the navy, Bill was "determined to never work in a building again" as he had done before. He felt he could escape the pain of working with others by working independently. He knew he had to create his own job and business if he was ever going to be able to support himself. With the help of his parents, he bought a tool truck with a well-known franchise and became an independent contractor who sold tools to auto mechanics. This was a perfect fit for Bill, as he was able to use his verbal strengths to sell tools, enabling him to become financially independent and live a comfortable life.

- ***Naive Natalie (Reading Nonverbal Social Cues)***

As a young adult, Natalie was really good at her job as a phone customer service representative. Jobs like this can be a good fit for NVLDers because it's all about verbal communication, which takes away the need to decode nonverbal communication. This was a position in which she could shine. The company had incentives and contests for employees to motivate them to reach their goals. Natalie was one of the few employees who consistently won. This helped to build her low self-esteem and gave her some confidence. Natalie worked at this job full-time for a few years before deciding to take advantage of their college tuition reimbursement program. She did such a good job that they created a part-time position for her to accommodate her school hours.

But one of the newer and younger supervisors didn't seem to like her. It was hard for her to discern this because of her NVLD. Some days, he seemed nice and others not. He asked her in front of all the other employees why she always acted like a dumb blonde. Natalie was embarrassed and flabbergasted. Looking back, she realized it was most likely due to her need to ask numerous questions during training workshops and difficulties with social pleasantries that made her stick out like a sore thumb.

One day, Natalie's supervisor called her into his office. He said he just wanted to check in with her to make sure she was all right. He told her if she ever needed anything, she could call him and gave her his personal phone number. This was puzzling to Natalie, as his behavior seemed so inconsistent. He was engaged at the time and knew his fiancée wouldn't make light of this, as his behavior was inappropriate.

A few weeks later, he began calling her into his office and telling her she wasn't doing her job correctly, which was untrue. He would present her with a document that stated that she was being disciplined; he expected her to sign it. Each time, she refused. During these "disciplinary sessions," he'd again give her his phone number—reminding her once again she could call him if she ever needed anything. He told her after three write-ups, the company would take action, and she could lose her job.

Never knowing when he would call her into his office or what she had supposedly done wrong made Natalie anxious. At the time, she didn't understand what he was doing because he didn't tell her verbally in words. He attempted, nonverbally, to box her into a corner by documenting false information and scaring her into believing she would lose her job. In exchange for him letting her keep her job, she would have to go along with his advances.

Natalie believed because she was regarded as an asset to the company and wasn't intimidated, her boss backed off. Even though she didn't realize what he was doing at the time, she knew her job performance was stellar. It didn't occur to her to go to the human resources department, as he was an authority figure, someone she was supposed to listen to. If you are unsure of how to read a situation, it's important to seek guidance and check it out with those you can trust to help you take the best course of action.

Who Knows Good Business Better than *Forbes?*

More and more, businesses, such as JP Morgan Chase, IBM, Microsoft, Goldman Sachs, CVS, Bank of America, and SAP Software Solutions, are starting to take notice and appreciate the value that neurodiversity brings to an organization. Benefits include higher levels of focused talent and better innovation. In the December 13, 2018, edition of *Forbes*, James Mahoney, then the head of JP Morgan's Autism at Work program, stated that autistic employees at JP Morgan achieve, on average, 48 percent to 140 percent more work than their typical colleagues.

In a 2018 op-ed for the *New York Times* called "Hiring People with Disabilities Is Good Business," Ted Kennedy Jr. says the idea that employees with disabilities would compromise a company's performance is conclusively wrong. Companies that hire people with disabilities realize revenues 28 percent higher on average, net income 200 percent higher, and increase profit margins by 30 percent. Companies that improved internal practices for disability inclusion were also four times more likely to see higher total shareholder returns. Research from Accenture says hiring just 1 percent of the 10.7 million people with disabilities has the potential to boost the GDP by an estimated $25 billion!

Of course, many people with NVLD already knew this. I was quoted in "Embrace Neurodiversity in the Workplace to Meet Your Business Needs," an article by Geoff Hoppe published in *Forbes* on June 10, 2020:

Because we've had so many challenges we've had to overcome, we're really good at solving problems and thinking outside the box. Everyday life is "a virtual training ground" for people with NVLD, often causing them to exceed expectations in the workplace. As a result, grit and perseverance are habitual to many employees with NVLD, which makes for solid employees.

Lessons Learned

- Explore neuropsychological evaluation options available to you.

- Know yourself. What do you like to do? What are you good at? What do you want to learn?

- Take advantage of career counseling services if they are available to you.

- Ensure you have the necessary education. Do you have the knowledge and the ability to accomplish the specific tasks of the job? If not, go back and fill in your knowledge gaps.

- Take stock of your social-emotional skills. Are you a good fit in this workplace? Do you want to improve your skills through this specific job? Do you understand how to manage workplace bullies?

- Read *Mapping Careers with LD and ADD Clients: Guidebook and Case Studies* by Raise Abby Janus.

- Gauge what kind of working environment would best fit your needs.
- Research companies before you interview with them.
- Make up a list of common questions interviewers ask about both you and your experience, and think about how you would be a good fit for this particular job.
- Role-play and film mock self-interviews.
- Know when to disclose your disability if at all. Should you do that before you are hired, after you are hired, or when you need assistance with accommodations? You will need to ask for accommodations before your probationary period on the job is over. Make sure you know when that is.
- Consider working for yourself. Do you have an interest in a particular area, such as providing a specific service or creating a product?
- Are your current skills sufficient for your job, or do you need more training? It may be easiest to begin to work with skills you already have.
- Use SCORE for free advice and support resources for small businesses, available at https://www.score.org.
- Make sure you add your own accommodations into your business plan so you take care of yourself while working to build your company.

Chapter 6

Friendships and Relationships

The inability to effectively process communication causes NVLDers to lag socially behind their peers. This clearly puts one at a disadvantage when it comes to making and maintaining relationships.

It wasn't until middle school that I figured out other kids got together outside of school. How would I know? No one ever directly said to me, "We get together outside of school." I longed for friends and a social life. I became severely depressed. I soothed myself by creating an alter ego to compensate for my loneliness and isolation. I'd imagine my phone ringing, chatting with friends, and being invited to parties and activities.

I attempted to connect with other kids by calling them on the phone several times a day. I had a list of kids I would contact (culled from the school directory, Girl Scout troop rosters, and acting classes). When I got to the end of the list, I would start calling again from the top of the list. Some kids put up with this and talked to me, but I never saw them in person outside of structured school and group activities. Often when I called others, I was told they were too busy to come to the phone or weren't home. I didn't understand that they did not want to talk to me and had no interest in being my friend, because they didn't explicitly tell me so. Unlike neurotypical children, I couldn't understand their nonverbal cues.

My childhood friend Lynne lived on my street and had a lot of friends. She usually included me in their get-togethers, and they were nice to me. Eventually I realized they were really more her friends than mine. To convince myself that I had friends, I would say the names of these kids and repeatedly count them on my fingers because this was soothing. I often could not stop this obsessive ritual until I reached the point of exhaustion.

After high school, these friends and the kids I had been surrounded by since grade school suddenly disappeared. Even though my peers weren't my friends they had been a part of my daily routine for years. Not knowing what to do with myself I would walk and drive around town looking for them, but I could not find them. It seemed as if everyone but me had moved on to the next stage of their lives (college or full-time jobs), leaving me in the dust. While I was desperately trying to find my way, I watched my peers move from one stage of life to the next—graduation, dating, boyfriends, jobs, college, careers, marriage, kids, promotions, and so on.

Marketing, Movies, TV Shows, and NVLDers

Marketing, movies, and TV shows can have both negative and positive effects on NVLDers. At younger ages, NVLDers can easily be swayed by their literal interpretations of marketing messages. These images triggered my feelings of inadequacy from childhood to my twenties. We often drove by a billboard advertising cigarettes with images of young people smoking and playing Frisbee on the beach, having a good time. As a result, I began smoking as an attempt to create the billboard scenario in my life.

Advertising works because it persuades people to buy products, but for people with NVLD who think literally, advertisements can become a guidebook for a good life. Before there were cell phones, Verizon offered a friends and family phone plan that was advertised on TV almost nonstop. The commercial showed groups of friends and family smiling, laughing, and having a good time together. Each time I saw this commercial, it triggered my feelings of sadness and inadequacy since I had so few friends and spent most of my time with my parents.

Although some movies and TV shows sometimes made me sad, they also helped me to learn social skills and to imagine a world where I was like everyone else. The actors on *The Brady Bunch*, *I Dream of Jeannie*, and *The Partridge Family* were like my friends. I could always count on them being there. When Marcia Brady or Keith Partridge experienced difficulties and learned how to solve their problems, I learned too. Today, I refer to TV shows like *Modern Family* and *The Fosters* that young people can watch and learn from. Parents, you can watch these shows with your kids as a springboard to discuss social problem-solving or turn the volume off and discuss the characters' nonverbal communication.

My mother noticed I was learning from these shows, so she decided to enroll me in acting class to help me make friends and build my self-confidence. These classes were priceless. They not only increased my self-esteem but gave me the courage to keep going in spite of tough times. I honed my abilities to mimic others using tone of voice, body language, character voices, and mannerisms. I had to practice these skills over and over again, which in turn improved my social interactions and confidence. But it wasn't foolproof. There were times when my actions and words didn't fit into the context of the situation, and I struggled.

> ### What Is Friendship?
> Friendship is a relationship between two people characterized by affection, respect, shared experiences and activities, emotional support, and equal standing. Determining who is and who isn't your friend can be challenging. Knowing the difference is vital to your success.

A friend is someone you really like, know well, respect, and trust, whereas an acquaintance is someone you know, have met, or do not know well. Interactions with acquaintances have little meaning in your life. However, because acquaintances come across as friendly, it can be difficult for NVLDers to know the difference.

It's important to recognize that though an acquaintance may appear to be like a true friend, that doesn't mean they actually are your friend. When an NVLDer mistakes an acquaintance for a friend, they may make themselves vulnerable to exploitation by the acquaintance.

If you don't have many friends, you may be excited about the prospect of a new friend and share too much personal information too quickly. The potential new friend may interpret your sharing confidential information as a sign of neediness and shy away from any further interaction.

Bide your time, and put in the effort it takes toward finding authentic friends. Keep on putting yourself out there, move on when you need to, and you will find your tribe! You can go to my Facebook support group, NVLD Pioneers, to find other like-minded people.

It Takes Time to Build Friendships

Jeffrey Hall, a communications professor at the University of Kansas, conducted a study on adults and friendships, and the results were published in the March 15, 2018, volume of the *Journal of Social and Personal Relationships*. According to Hall, you need to spend about fifty hours with someone before you consider them a casual friend, ninety hours before you become real friends, and about two hundred hours to become close friends. Results suggest that the chance of transitioning from casual

> friend to friend is greater than 50 percent after around eighty to one hundred hours together. Parents, use this information to help your children understand how big an investment you need to make to develop friendships.

Frenemies

A frenemy is someone who seems to be a friend but who actually resents or dislikes you. They can be fun to spend time with and offer support and encouragement until they get what they need through your interactions. Sometimes they may feel jealous of you or behave competitively toward you when you seem to be doing well.

Frenemies come in all ages, shapes, and sizes, from elementary school to the boardroom. They form alliances with mutual friends to sway those people's opinions of you and push you out of the friendship circle. When they are unsuccessful in their attempts to isolate you from others, they resort to becoming your frenemy to preserve their social standing in the group.

People who pose as frenemies are skilled at deception. Given their difficulty with nonverbal communication, NVLDers and NDs can be easily manipulated by frenemies without knowing it. In fact, even neurotypicals often struggle to identify frenemies because they are adept at hiding their agendas. It's important to teach children that no matter what someone says, they may not be telling the truth. Remind them that actions speak louder than words.

James and the Onion

I'll never forget James, an elementary school student in my special education class who was desperate for friends. A group of boys used this knowledge and posed as his friends in order to make fun of him for their own entertainment.

One day during lunch, one of the boys gave James an onion and told him he could eat it like an apple. James always sat by himself during lunchtime, and since this boy was sharing food with him, he took this as a sign that they wanted to be friends. Even though he knew better than to eat the onion, knowing it would taste horrible and be an unpleasant experience, he was desperate to have friends.

Because of James's difficulties deciphering tone of voice (sarcasm) and nonverbal communication, he fell into their trap, believing they wanted to be friends and just wanted to have a good time with him. As he was gagging on the onion and his eyes were tearing, the boys turned on him and began calling him names. It was only then that he finally understood, from their words, that they were making fun of him. James was so humiliated he broke down in tears and ran out of the cafeteria.

If you've seen the movie *Mean Girls*, based on the book *Queen Bees and Wannabes* by Rosalind Wiseman, you know exactly what I'm talking about. No matter how hard she tries, Cady Heron—the new girl in high school—can't make friends. Cady cannot process and understand nonverbal communication and is unaware of the social dynamics of cliques and unwritten rules like what you wear determines who you hang out with. If you are the parent of a teenage daughter, *Mean Girls* will help you understand the dynamics of social relationships among girls. Watching the movie with your daughter can help her to feel understood. *A Smart Girl's Guide to Friendship Troubles: Dealing with Fights, Being Left Out, and the Whole Popularity Thing* by Patti Kelley Criswell is another good resource for adolescent girls.

Point Break, starring Patrick Swayze and Keanu Reeves, is an action-crime movie that can also help teen boys and girls understand the concept of frenemies. FBI Agent Keanu Reeves is assigned to infiltrate a group of surfers who are suspected of robbing banks. Parents, you may want to watch this film in advance of sharing it with your children. *Diary of a 6th Grade Ninja 10: My Worst Frenemy* by Marcus Emerson is a good read for boys in fourth grade and up to help them better understand and cope with frenemies.

Cutting Your Losses

If you don't feel good about yourself when you are with your friends, pay attention to those feelings. If you feel anxious, defensive, criticized, unsupported, or used, it's time to let those friends go. I kept fair-weather and toxic friends longer than I should have because I was lonely. Eventually,

I learned how to pick and choose my friends by not settling for less than what I deserved. Leaving behind these types of so-called friends was crucial to my emotional well-being.

Samantha knew her friend wasn't always reliable, but because she had no other friends and nothing else to do, she went out dancing with the friend one night. When Samantha's friend ran into an acquaintance who invited her to leave the bar and go to a party, Samantha was left by herself without a ride home. Had she cut her losses earlier, Samantha wouldn't have endured this painful experience.

Trusting Your Gut, Asking for Help, and Leaving the Door Open

Your gut instinct is the intuitive knowledge, coming from your solar plexus or diaphragm, that gives you the confidence to trust your assessment of a situation even if you can't figure it out with information and facts. You can ask trusted friends how they might feel if they were in your shoes to get a point of reference that will help you to ascertain if you're sizing up the situation correctly and formulate a response. See how Kim, one of my clients, handled a situation using this technique.

Trusting Your Feelings and Keeping Doors Open

Kim, a forty-five-year-old woman with NVLD, belonged to a women's group that met for an hour each week to celebrate sisterhood through fun activities. During the pandemic, the women continued to meet online via Zoom. Since Kim was the only member of the group who knew how to use the Zoom platform, Mia, the group's leader, asked her to send out the invites. Kim really enjoyed doing this and felt more a part of the group until she received a group text to look for a Zoom invite from Donna for their next meeting.

Kim didn't know what had transpired and had been planning to send out the invites that day. She wanted to question this but didn't know if it was appropriate to do so. She became extremely anxious and played the situation over and over in her mind. Did I miss something? Was Mia mad at me because I couldn't always do 7:00 p.m. meetings? If I tell her I am upset, will I come across as petty? Kim doubted herself because of the many times she hadn't sized up situations correctly. She desperately wanted to work this out on her own, but she also realized that she needed help interpreting the situation and finding the best way to handle it.

She checked it out with two trusted friends who both said they would have felt brushed aside and would want to know why. However, they differed in how they would handle the situation: one said she would bring it up in conversation, while the other said she would let it go. I suggested that she make her decision based on her gut—what felt right to her. Although she didn't have all the facts, Kim's instinct told her that some of the women had deeper friendships and that this was at the root of the confusion.

I helped her to resolve the situation in a way that would empower her, be a win-win for everyone, and be a model for how to handle similar situations in the future. She decided to talk to Mia to clarify what was going on. Mia had said she forgot and that Kim could set up the Zoom meeting for next week. However, the following week, Kim received another invite from Donna to the Zoom meeting, which prompted her to text Mia.

> **Kim to Mia:** I'm confused. You told me I was doing the Zoom meeting this week. Is there a reason why you switched to Donna setting it up instead of me? As I said earlier, I enjoy it, as it makes me feel more part of the group since I don't know everyone as the others do.

> **Mia:** There is no reason. Donna volunteered, so I just went with that. She uses Zoom for her work too.

Kim: Oh, I guess I didn't volunteer, as I thought I was already doing it. Honestly, my feelings are hurt. I expressed how it made me feel a part of the group. Now I feel pushed aside.

Mia: Oh, my gosh, relax. Please don't make this into a thing. Donna and I have been friends for years. We talk every day. We have done this group together for many years. She is as familiar with Zoom as you are. I guess I felt it was no big deal.

Mia had "forgotten" that Donna initially didn't know how to use Zoom and had asked Kim to set up the meetings. At this point, Kim wasn't interested in playing this game any longer. It would only make it look as if she was competing with Donna. Her gut instinct had been confirmed. Mia and Donna were tight friends, and that was what was really going on. It also seemed that Donna didn't like her doing the meetings and was trying to engage her in a power struggle. She decided to let it go.

Kim: I'm glad she learned how to do it.

When Kim opened the email for the next meeting, she noticed that Donna had scheduled the meetings for the next two months—another affirmation that she wanted to be in charge. Kim was terribly hurt, and her first reaction was to drop out of the group. However, she chose to continue to attend the meetings. This was progress for Kim. She didn't burn her bridges. She left the door open. It was a good thing too! A few weeks later, Mia contacted Kim to offer Kim's husband, a contractor, the opportunity to bid on a construction project, which he won, providing much-needed income for the family.

Through her work with me, Kim was able to take steps to address the situation in a healthy way, let go of her angry feelings, validate her gut instincts, and keep the door open to possible opportunities and relationships. She realized that while Mia was inconsiderate, that behavior didn't warrant her walking away from the group. She eventually developed a deeper friendship with one of the women and continued to enjoy the meetings. Kim was proud of herself for trusting her feelings and getting help to resolve the situation in the best possible way.

Exercise: Trusting Your Gut

When you feel anxious, your mind can spin and ruminate on thoughts that may leave you feeling scattered and unsure of yourself. However, your body is always sending signals to guide you if you pay attention to them.

Think about trying on a new pair of shoes before purchasing them. You don't really think about whether they are a good fit for you, you feel it. If the shoes are too tight, pinch your toes, or are too loose around your heels, you know they are not a good fit for you. Your body, not your mind, has sent you the signals to come to this conclusion.

Try this exercise to learn how to listen to your gut instincts. Sit or lie down in a quiet place. Take a deep breath, and bring your attention to your body to see what feelings come up. How do you feel when you are with this person? Are you happy? Do you feel tense? If a conflict has strained your friendship, how do you feel about what has transpired?

Really feel the emotion without judging it. Although you may feel foolish doing this, ask your gut about the situation in question. Your body will communicate with you. Tune into your inner voice, and you will know what to do.

It takes some practice to learn to do this, but keep at it, and you'll be able to use this technique to balance out what your thoughts and body are telling you. You'll learn more about holistic techniques in the "Mind, Body, Spirit" chapter.

Taking Things at Face Value

The issue of trust is complicated for many with NVLD because they tend to interpret words literally. Many clients have told me that they were completely unaware they had been taken advantage of, saying, "That's not what I was told," "He didn't say that," or "I didn't think that was what she meant." For NVLDers, words are their truth guide, which is why it is so important for them to learn social skills to compensate for their difficulties processing nonverbal communication.

One consequence of literal thinking is being easily swayed by the opinions of others. Take Tanya, one of my high school clients, who had a reputation for being "two-faced." One day, her friend Sophie asked her to go to the movies with her. She described the film she had chosen and why they should see it. When Tanya invited Gabrielle to join them, Gabrielle dismissed this film and told Tanya why they should see another film instead. Tanya told Sophie they were going to see Gabrielle's choice. Sophie accused Tanya of being "two-faced" because this wasn't the first time Tanya had changed their plans at someone else's request.

Tanya felt overwhelmed and confused, not knowing how to respond because at the moment when each of her friends expressed their movie preferences, it all "sounded so right." With my help, Tanya was better able to handle social situations like these.

Social Pleasantries

Social pleasantries convey friendliness and ease into conversations. When acquaintances ask "How are you?" it's a formality we are expected to answer with lines like "Great. How about you?" No one really wants to know how you are doing unless they are someone close to you with a vested interest. NVLDers may misinterpret such courtesy questions and answer them literally.

Whenever Amanda was asked, "How are you?" she'd answer with details about everything going on in her life. If she wasn't feeling well, she'd go into detail listing all of her ailments. If she was upset about something, she would explain what happened and share her feelings about it. She might even ask for advice. Unbeknown to her, she made others feel uncomfortable, pushing them away from her. Once Amanda learned the ins and outs of social pleasantries, she was better able to blend in and be accepted by others.

Disclosing to Friends, Acquaintances, and Family

Do you tell people you have NVLD? Does disclosure help people to better understand you or not? Does it increase isolation and nonacceptance?

I wish I had a crystal ball and could give you the answer, but there are no right answers when it comes to disclosing. Some of my clients have said that others are more understanding and forgiving of their gaffes when they learn about NVLD. Many have said that it has made things worse. Unfortunately, there will always be those who think you are using the label as an excuse. It's possible that instead of the hoped-for outcome of empathy and understanding, you've opened the door to even more rejection. Ultimately, only you can decide what the best decision is given the situation. Each situation has its own set of circumstances to consider. You could offer this book to people if you feel they may be receptive to learning more about NVLD.

You Don't Get a Pass

Lisa and Katie had been acquaintances for years before they found themselves working at the same company. Gradually, as the women got to know their coworkers, they were invited to lunch, after-work happy hours, dinner parties, and other activities. Lisa was thrilled to find herself included, as she had had great difficulty managing friendships since grade school. She had made so much progress, having worked hard throughout the years to compensate for her weak nonverbal communication skills. Having been burned from past disclosures, Lisa did what the majority of NVLDers do: she "masked" to pass as neurotypical. She described it as "walking on eggshells" and was constantly bracing herself for when "the rug would be pulled out from under my feet."

At lunch one day, the women, including Katie, were sitting together talking and laughing. When Lisa approached them, they abruptly stopped talking, but not before she had overheard that the conversation was about a get-together that she had not been invited to. She felt a wave of anxiety as memories of her painful past came rushing back. She pushed back her tears and put on her happy face before she excused herself. Later in the week, while perusing Facebook, Lisa found proof that her "friends" had gotten together without her many times.

Lisa knew she was having trouble navigating the group's dynamics. She wasn't sure she was picking up on all the social cues. Since she knew Katie and felt comfortable with her, she reached out to her to ask for help in understanding why she was being left out. She sent Katie an email, explained that she had NVLD, and attached an article about it. She asked if she had done anything to offend her or any of the women and stated that, if so, it wasn't intentional. Lisa explained that she sometimes misunderstands the implications of nonverbal communication, which can leave others confused by her behavior.

When Lisa didn't hear back from Katie, she called her. Katie listed all the things she did that were offensive to others and gave her an earful, saying, "You are no different than anyone else; you are looking for special attention, are self-centered, and are playing the victim. Shouting your

NVLD from the rooftops isn't going to get you the pass you are looking for. You need to suck it up."

This conversation with Katie sent Lisa into a downward spiral of depression that lasted for months. She spent endless hours overanalyzing and replaying the situations in her mind, trying to figure out what she had missed and what she could have done differently.

Social Exclusion: Intentional or Unintentional?

Social exclusion—now known as canceling—is the intentional act of ostracizing individuals, denying them the social connectivity that's essential to their well-being. Lisa was intentionally left out by this group of women. However, social exclusion isn't rejection when it's unintentional, such as when friends spontaneously get together, and it just happened to work out for any number of reasons that you were unintentionally excluded. So, don't always assume you have been excluded when it was "just the way things worked out." Remember, you don't have to be NVLD to be unintentionally excluded, as it happens to everyone!

In this case, Katie was unable to see Lisa's difficulties stemming from NVLD. She looked at Lisa from her own vantage point: Katie's problems were, in her mind, on the same level as Lisa's. NDs and NTs experience some of the same difficulties we all face in life, including social rejection. However, the intensity and frequency of the situations and the degree of chronic struggles is different. Unfortunately, Katie couldn't or wouldn't see Lisa's difficulties in the context of the brain-based learning deficit that made it harder for her to navigate the social dynamics of relationships. After all, Lisa didn't *look* like she had a disability. This was a case where the situation went downhill upon disclosure.

NVLDers can be anxious about making the wrong decisions or sharing too much too soon. Many people have shared with me that after they disclosed their disability, others doubted their capabilities, which negatively affected friendships. Make the best decisions for yourself without guilt or regret.

It's also important to learn about the different types of friendships in the workplace and to understand that even though you are meeting outside of work, it's not a given that these people are your friends. Hybrid friendships (work and personal) require good boundaries and strong social-emotional skills. If you decide to pursue these friendships, be cautious and take it slow. You may choose to limit these types of friendships by being friendly and attending selective events. Having your own circle of trusted friends outside of work is much safer and won't put you in uncomfortable situations on the job.

Lessons Learned

- Know that your feelings are not right or wrong.
- Ask for help from established, trustworthy friends on how to handle troubling situations.
- Weigh your options before disclosing your NVLD to acquaintances or strangers. You can let people know your communication style—what works best for you—without disclosing you have NVLD.
- Know that attending an activity consistently with others doesn't mean everyone is automatically your friend.
- Don't expect to make a friend in every group you try.
- It's perfectly normal to see some people solely in the group setting and not outside that one activity. If you make one friend, it's a bonus.
- Keep putting yourself out there, and you will find your way and learn from your experiences.
- Realize it takes time for friendships to develop.
- You don't need a ton of friends. Aim for two to five, as you don't want to rely on one person to meet all of your social needs.
- One-on-one friendships have much to offer and may be easier to manage. You don't need to be part of a group to have a fulfilling social life.

- Enroll yourself or your child in acting classes. It's not only fun but a great way to improve your skills and make friends.
- Remember that actions speak louder than words. Actions demonstrate a person's true intentions more effectively than words.
- Learn about the norms and expectations of "social pleasantries."
- Trust your gut, and take appropriate action.
- Join my NVLD Pioneers Facebook group to meet like-minded people at https://www.facebook.com/NvldPioneers.

CHAPTER 7

Masking and the Struggle for Emotional Well-Being

Every day, individuals with NVLD and NDs are living in pain from the effects of being misunderstood. These children and adults battle to preserve their self-esteem at home, at school, at work, and in their relationships. Many are in a perpetual defensive mode, on alert for many of their waking hours to protect themselves from real or perceived attacks. There is no break, time off, or holiday away from NVLD. Receiving relentless misinterpretation and negative feedback is like having a scab repeatedly pulled off a wound that then never heals.

Dozens of studies have revealed that being misunderstood, devalued, bullied, and judged as a child leads to low self-esteem, lack of confidence, feelings of worthlessness, anxiety, depression, and trauma, which in turn leads to marginalization and significant mental health challenges. Here are some of the things I've heard from children and adults throughout my professional tenure:

- "I tried so hard, and it doesn't do any good, so why bother?"
- "I thought I was retarded."
- "No one likes me. I am a bad person."

- "Why can't I ever do anything right?"
- "People think I am trying to give them a hard time and that I am arguing with them."
- "I'm doing my best to understand others, but it doesn't matter; they are always mad at me."
- "I wish I was never born."
- "I wish they would know I'm not a bad person."
- "What am I doing wrong to be treated like this?"
- "I feel like I'm in court every day, defending myself."
- "I wish I knew what was wrong with me."
- "Why doesn't anyone like me?"
- "I feel like a cruel joke is being played on me."
- "I can't learn. I am dumb and stupid."

To cover up the pain of being misunderstood, NVLD'ers often develop masks to divert attention away from their deficits, save themselves from embarrassment, and avoid criticism. When we mask to hide who we are to fit in, we lose our authentic selves, but sometimes it's the only way to survive in a neurotypical world.

Since there is no research on masking and its emotional impact on NVLDers, I've relied on the research demonstrating the high rates of "camouflaging" among autistic individuals. "Masking" is exhausting and can negatively affect mental and physical health. The chronic cognitive engagement involved in masking can lead to meltdowns, social overload, anxiety, and depression. I've seen many who struggle with headaches, gastrointestinal issues, and other ailments from masking.

What about those in the autistic community who are told, "You don't look autistic." It's as if they are being congratulated for doing such a good job of camouflaging themselves to be accepted by NTs. Remember the excruciating pain Lisa experienced when she was excluded from social gatherings at work and how hard she worked to appear neurotypical? Remember my yearning for acceptance from others? What is unknown to NTs is the amount of effort it takes to hide neurodivergence. Many NVLDers get pushback from people who don't believe them, which puts them in a position to defend or prove themselves.

A mask I used frequently during my school years was sickness. The stress-related ulcers I developed, which were an acceptable reason to stay home from school, showed me I could use this ruse to escape other painful situations. I also used this mask when the math teacher called students to the blackboard. I'd tell the teacher I didn't feel well and needed to go to the nurse's office.

Maskers can be dramatic, putting on a show of holding their stomachs, limping, putting their head down on the desk, and so on. I have seen many different masks worn over the years (sweet-talkers, know-it-alls, nonconformists, people-pleasers, one-uppers, victims, and more) used to hide their vulnerabilities in exchange for acceptance. Unfortunately, these tactics often backfire and push others away instead of giving them the validation they crave.

Rejection Sensitivity Dysphoria (RSD)

By age twelve, children with ADHD have received twenty thousand more negative messages from parents, teachers, and other adults than twelve-year-olds without ADHD, according to research conducted by psychiatrist William Dodson and reported on www.chadd.org (July 18, 2019). While we don't yet have the numbers for NVLD, it's not a stretch to assume it's a similar number or higher. Their over-the-top reactions may lead you to believe that your NVLD student, child, or spouse is being unreasonable, overly sensitive, or defiant. In reality, their responses have been shaped by years of negative messages, rejections, criticism, and bullying. In my work, I have seen that this abuse often results in the NVLDers developing rejection sensitivity dysphoria (RSD).

Though RSD is still not fully understood by scientists, many believe it is caused by multiple factors, including a history of parental rejection in childhood, bullying, criticism, and rejection in romantic relationships. Although symptoms of RSD can mimic other conditions, such as depression, RSD symptoms are usually brief and arise from the NVLDer's emotional state rather than an actual event. Almost all of my students and clients with NVLD have varying degrees of RSD. Like NVLD, RSD is not yet an official disorder listed in the *DSM*.

When NTs do not recognize their nonverbal communication is not understood by NVLDers, they make erroneous judgments about the NVLDers. It only takes so many accusations for a person to develop hypersensitivity to being misread or misunderstood. Social rejection, which is activated in the same brain area as physical pain, can be even more painful than physical injury or illness.

> ### Denise
> Linda helped me understand that certain situations—like concentrating for long periods at school or work or socializing—can be physically and mentally draining for individuals with ADHD. It is OK, and necessary, for them to need to take time to unwind or rest alone after situations that are stressful for them.

When my eighteen-year-old daughter would act out in anger or disrespect, Linda suggested I visualize her as a ten-year-old little girl in pigtails. Since she was emotionally immature for her age, that would help me reduce my expectations. I could see that my daughter was experiencing RSD, that she was frustrated or overwhelmed and was not able to handle or react appropriately to the situation. Linda's advice allowed me to step back and find the patience to help her. Controlling my reaction to her behavior was helpful for both of us.

Self-Blame and Self-Doubt
Years ago, a child in my special education class suddenly began seeing and hearing things that seemed to be real. After

he showed me where he saw a man hanging from the ceiling in the school hallway, I realized that he was experiencing auditory and visual hallucinations. Shortly afterward, he told me he didn't want to live anymore.

Any professional should take talk of suicide seriously, and in New Jersey, professionals, such as teachers and social workers, are mandated to report it to the state child abuse hotline. I went to speak with the principal, who was out for the day. I was directed to speak with a language arts teacher who was taking her place. He told me, "Don't worry about it; there's nothing we can do. Don't call."

I called the New Jersey Department of Children and Families (DYFS) anyway. The child was immediately taken to a crisis center by a crisis mobile response team. His intake evaluation indicated that he was mentally unstable. He was hospitalized, placed on medication, and diagnosed with schizophrenia.

The following day, I was chastised by five administrators who grilled me on the events of the past day and reprimanded me for disregarding the order to not contact DYFS. Later, the school district superintendent discovered that the administration had acted irresponsibly by not following mental health protocols and exchanged harsh words with the staff. Interestingly, the superintendent never acknowledged me for standing up to the administration and following the proper protocol for the protection and welfare of this child. A fellow teacher informed me that if the superintendent had done so, he would have been admitting wrongdoing on their part. If I had filed a complaint, the school would be held accountable.

I knew that I did the right thing, yet I was plagued by self-doubt and wondered if I had done something wrong. Someone did finally tell me that I was being blamed in an effort by the administrators to protect themselves and the school from liability. It's so easy to go into self-blame after years of repeated misunderstandings and angry, negative feedback. After this incident, I was traumatized. I blamed myself because I was *verbally* told I was at fault.

The Law of Large Numbers

It was a math concept, of all things, that helped me to understand that not everything I experienced was my fault. The law of large numbers helped me to think clearly and objectively. It was a tool I could use to stop myself from getting sucked into the black hole of self-blame. According to the law, the greater the number of experiences a person has, the more likely the outcome of wrong interpretations will be closer to fifty-fifty. In other words, it is statistically impossible for you to be wrong all the time.

One of the most important ways to improve your chances of making a correct assumption or decision is to expand your understanding of social situations through social skills training. Remember, it's not just the number of events but the unknown variables in each specific situation (including the mood, opinions, and experiences of others) that influence the outcomes. Emotions, like worry about being perceived as incompetent, play a big role in any specific event. By learning to recognize the weak points in your own decision-making process, you will improve your chance of making the right choice next time.

Learned Helplessness

According to psychologist Martin Seligman, learned helplessness originates from feelings of powerlessness, which are the result of persistent failure and trauma. Learned helplessness, which can lead to or exacerbate depression, is increasingly common and prevalent in our world.

I see many individuals of all ages who have developed learned helplessness as a result of their parents doing too much for them. Parents feel bad that things are so hard for them. The fact is life is harder for those with NVLD than for NTs, and even more challenging for undiagnosed NVLDers. Providing guidance and assistance to your child who is struggling isn't the same as doing too much for them. Ignore the feedback you get from others who think you are babying your child who is not performing on the same level as their peers socially, emotionally, or behaviorally. NVLD children develop more slowly than NT kids. They will catch up, but it will take time.

Your child needs your help and guidance to meet developmental milestones. There will be times when you will need to advocate for your child, but that is not the same as doing things for them that they can learn to do for themselves. Pairing guidance, protection, and instruction will give your child the tools to better cope as they grow and develop.

When parents do too much for their children, the children are robbed of the opportunity to learn how to manage on their own. They learn that if tasks are too hard for them, they should not bother trying. Waiting until they are adolescents makes this teaching more difficult because teens are not as open to being guided. By then, they have built up resentment and anger due to their unresolved difficulties from an earlier age. Unfortunately, most of these kids will learn the hard way when they hit rock bottom in adulthood before they are willing to seek help.

Separation Anxiety

After high-school graduation, I lived in constant fear because I had no idea how I would support myself. I knew some people who moved into apartments with friends and shared the rent. I didn't really know how to make and keep friends or have the life skills to manage my life. I had so many obstacles to overcome—depression, anxiety, panic attacks, lack of life and social skills, inability to maintain employment—that living on my own seemed impossible. I was terrified I would be unable to care for myself and would one day wind up living on the street.

When I started college, I shared an apartment on campus. Nonetheless I sought the comfort of my home and my parents and drove to their house in between classes. Panic seemed to be taking over my life. I often feared that if my parents died, I would have no way to survive. It isn't unusual for adult NVLDers to rely on parents to meet their basic needs. Many need to live at home, as it's overwhelming to function and meet neurotypical demands independently.

Within the NVLD population, there are those who will need assistance to meet their basic needs. According to psychologist Abraham Maslow, every human has the same basic need for food, shelter, clothing, safety, love, belonging, esteem, and self-actualization. Some NVLDers will take longer to fulfill each of those needs but will eventually become independent, while others will always need ongoing support.

Thankfully there are many parents of adult children who are willing to provide many of those needs while helping them to become independent. The road may be a little rocky, but with support, determination, and training, they can succeed. Others, like David, who had a supportive mother but a father who did not understand the impact of his deficits, have a struggle ahead of them. Many parents have unrealistic expectations of what their child can do on their own. But things did turn out well for David, as you'll see in his story.

Meet David

When I met David, he was a twenty-five-year-old college graduate who was unemployed and living with his parents. His father was on the verge of kicking David out of the house because he had not even found an entry-level job and was living at home to take advantage of the perks his parents provided, like internet service and free food. David's mom recognized his difficulties but was also part of the problem. She did so much for him that David never learned life skills.

His dad gave him an ultimatum to come and see me or get out. Since he had no way of supporting himself and his options were limited, he reluctantly agreed to work with me. He presented as an emotionally delayed, immature teenager without insight into his behavior and denied that he needed help. He thought his parents were "nags." He and his friends spent a lot of time getting high and playing music.

Once I began working with David, it was apparent that he had NVLD. It took some time for his dad to buy into the assessment. When students do not draw attention to themselves through behavior problems, they often slip through the cracks. When they struggle with academics but are compliant, likable, and try hard, their learning disabilities disappear under the radar too. David's father needed to release his disappointment about his son's behaviors and his mother needed to cut the apron strings in order for David to develop the skills of independence.

David, his parents, and I worked together to build up his self-esteem. I focused on helping him to develop his weak processing skills, including visual, auditory, active working memory, logic and reasoning, and processing speed. As a result, David was then better able to use strategies and tools to manage his time and projects. David learned to use his phone for reminders, developed systems to manage his paperwork, mastered interpretation of social cues, held down a job, and chose healthier friends. He cut back on marijuana consumption because he realized it was killing his motivation. When he started working for a food delivery company, he gave his parents money for rent and expenses and became a contributing member of the household. Thanks to the understanding and support of his parents, David no longer needs to worry about having a roof over his head. His anxiety has diminished, and he feels safer. However, because of his NVLD, he still has employment issues and needs ongoing support to understand the meaning of communications at work. David has matured and is willing to do the work it takes to get the life he wants.

Codependency

Healthy caretaking involves reciprocal behaviors within a relationship. We make sacrifices by giving up something to please or help someone, such as going to a movie we'd rather not see, passing up on invitations in order to be available for a friend in need, and rearranging our schedules to take someone to a doctor's appointment. For example, my friend appreciated my support when she was sick, and the next time we went to dinner together, she ordered a low-calorie dish to help me stay on my diet.

Initially, children are totally dependent on their parents or caregivers to meet their basic needs as they develop and become independent. When adults with NVLD are unable to meet their own needs, their relationships become codependent.

"Codependent relationships signify a degree of unhealthy clinginess when one person isn't self-sufficient or autonomous," says Scott Wetzler, PhD, psychology division chief at Albert Einstein College of Medicine. "One or both parties depend on their loved ones for fulfillment.[2]"

Unfortunately, people with invisible disabilities, like NVLD, typically are not recognized as having legitimate dependency needs. Some people look down on people like David, labeling them as irresponsible or taking advantage of others.

---

[2] (Sun, Feifei. "Are You in a Codependent Relationship?" WebMD.com, 7 August 2014, https://www.webmd.com/sex-relationships/features/signs-of-a-codependent-relationship)

The concept and scope of codependency are so broad that it goes beyond the confines of this book. Although there is much information about codependency, particularly as it relates to children and adults from dysfunctional families and those with drug or alcohol addictions, there is very little research on codependency and people with learning disabilities. The sole purpose of discussing codependency in this book is to highlight how it relates to those with NVLD.

A Double-Edged Sword

Just like a drowning person frantically grabs for anything to stay afloat, NVLDers often attach themselves to anyone who can help them make sense out of their chaotic world. Is it any wonder then that many find themselves in unhealthy relationships to get their needs met? The cold reality is that codependency can be a necessary evil for adults with insufficient skills and little or no family support.

While it certainly isn't ideal to be codependent, it is often a matter of physical or emotional survival. Had David's father been unable to acknowledge his adult son's inability to meet his own needs, he could have ended up out on the street and homeless. Sadly, for those diagnosed as neurodivergent in their adult years, unhealthy relationships are usually the norm. Forming healthy relationships with people who possess the skills to support their growing independence is critical for those with NVLD.

There are many advantages to being diagnosed with NVLD in childhood. The diagnosis gives parents the permission to teach their children how to choose and navigate healthy relationships. This, along with social and life skills interventions and other supports, can lessen the occurrence of negative codependent relationships.

Covert Abuse

Codependent NVLDers are at risk of emotional, physical, sexual, and financial abuse. Abusers are often seen by others as helpful, competent, and caring, making it even more confusing to identify the abuser's underlying goal of total control. Wolves in sheep's clothing, they seek to gain their victim's trust, and once they do, their abuse begins to happen so gradually that it feels normal to the individual who is abused. For people with NVLD communications challenges, it may be very difficult to recognize when their boundaries are violated and they are being abused.

Gaslighting is an emotionally abusive tactic that abusers use to make their victims question their feelings and thoughts—and even their sanity. Over time, the abused person loses self-esteem, self-confidence, and clarity as to what is real. This type of abuse is so insidious that even neurotypicals can have difficulty identifying when they are being abused. It would take those with NVLD much longer to see the reality of this kind of abuse, to read the behavior of the wolf, in comparison to their neurotypical peers.

Exploitation

One of the wonderful qualities of NVLDers is compassion for others, thanks to their first-hand experience of what it feels like to be the underdog. Many would give the shirt off their backs to help someone in need. I've worked with kids and adults who are so kindhearted they have started food drives, collected blankets for the homeless, and have raised money for other charitable causes. However, they can be exploited by manipulative people.

NVLDers don't always recognize when exploitation is occurring. They lend money and pay for meals, gas, and entertainment because they believe that this is how a friend behaves. One parent shared that even though they had warned their daughter not to be generous with her boyfriend's family, she continually gave them money because she was desperate for attention and acceptance.

Not knowing whether they are reading people and the situation correctly impacts NVLDers' ability to respond to others. This is why it's so important for parents and educators to explicitly teach children what is appropriate and inappropriate behavior on the part of others, regardless of the words spoken. Recognizing the signs of exploitation and abuse are critical life skills.

Loneliness and Fear

The anxiety from second-guessing how they came across to others can contribute to NVLDers' loneliness. Fear begins to take over, and soon you're reliving scenarios of all the mistakes you made or imagining ones you will make in the future. In an attempt to understand what's happening, many obsessively analyze past events and conversations to identify why things turned out so bad. Though worrying fools your mind into thinking you're productive, in fact, these ruminating thoughts increase anxiety.

To cope with their difficulties, NVLDers tend to isolate themselves to protect themselves. However, removing oneself from further interactions is an ineffective strategy. Some NVLDers may verbally offer too much information too soon to compensate for their poor nonverbal skills, which can cause others to feel uncomfortable or disinterested in getting to know them better.

Adults with a learning disability are seven times as likely as their nondisabled peers to be lonely, and as many as 30 percent of those adults aged eighteen to thirty-five spend less than an hour outside their homes on a typical Saturday, according to a 2016 survey by Mencap, a UK-based advocacy organization for people with learning disabilities. Another study published in the April 27, 2016, issue of the *Journal of Intellectual Disability Research* revealed that children and teenagers with a learning disability partake in fewer activities and participate less frequently than their peers without a learning disability. They also tend to have fewer friends.

We all need to feel cared for, loved, and accepted in our relationships with friends, family, romantic partners, and coworkers. Our brains are wired for social connection. There have been numerous studies showing that those who are socially active are happier, live longer, and have better physical health. Fortunately, NVLDers can learn to make these connections.

A New Normal

I began writing this book three months into the global coronavirus pandemic. As I am about to finish the book, we are still in the middle of the social-emotional upheaval the pandemic caused. For those first few months, people were happy to stay at home in their pajamas binging on Netflix. But as the pandemic stretched through into its third year, more and more people became depressed and anxious as they coped with homeschooling, staying healthy, earning income, feeding their families, and paying the bills while dealing with an uncertain future.

Social media has been flooded with stories of how lonely and isolated people are. I'm sure many of you can relate to the effects of the COVID virus and the new feelings of loneliness. This may be the very first time that many people have been isolated from family, friends, or coworkers.

Long before the pandemic, feelings of loneliness and isolation were very familiar to the majority of NVLD and ND individuals. NTs are now experiencing many of the same issues and difficulties as NDs—extreme stress, social isolation, uncertainty, lack of information, anxiety, and needing to solve problems in unconventional ways. Ironically, what

I'm seeing among those in the neurodiverse community is that not much has changed in their daily lives, so they are coping much better in comparison to NTs. For the first time, many NVLDers have recognized their strength and resilience and no longer feel excluded from their peer group. They are saying, "Welcome to my world," and are feeling less stigmatized because of their deficits.

The isolation and anxiety experienced during COVID will eventually fade as we get back to normal. However, for approximately 1.3 billion people with learning disabilities, this loneliness will remain their norm.

Although most people may not like living with loneliness and isolation, NVLDers often prefer it. Living and working in isolation can provide somewhat of a safe haven since it minimizes the interactions that cause embarrassment, shame, and rejection. Not having to be on guard, mask, or walk on eggshells becomes a relief. Although it's not what they would have chosen for themselves, it's the lesser of two evils. The payoff of safety and self-protection outweighs their loneliness.

Nevertheless, the safety they seek prevents them from enjoying life. The good news is they don't need to suffer from isolation and loneliness. They can find and create a balance. You'll learn more about this in the next chapter.

NVLD, Co-occurring Conditions, and Mental Health

It's not uncommon for stress stemming from NVLD to compromise one's mental health. I developed severe depression and obsessive-compulsive disorder (OCD). Many NVLDers develop OCD thoughts and behaviors in an attempt to control the chronic and overwhelming difficulties of coping with NVLD. Some of my NVLD clients have also been diagnosed with dependent personality disorder (DPD), attention deficit hyperactivity disorder (ADHD), oppositional defiant disorder (ODD), and borderline personality disorder (BPD). There is a lot of overlap in the symptoms and behaviors of NVLD, DPD, ADHD, ODD, and BPD, which often leads to a misdiagnosis.

I believe that behaviors that lead to these diagnoses are triggered by the intense anxiety of being unable to comprehend nonverbal communication, which affects the ability to effectively perform socially and emotionally in all areas of life. Although this isn't something that has been fully acknowledged by medical professionals, it's my opinion that the symptoms mistaken for OCD, ADHD, DPD, and BPD can be a result of trying to cope with NVLD.

I successfully hid my symptoms from my parents. When I was floundering, my parents sent me for counseling because that was all they knew to do. Because I was so well-spoken, the therapist did not believe the extent of my distress. However, she did refer me to someone who diagnosed me with OCD, which in my case was triggered by the ramifications of living with NVLD. The doctor showed me a video describing the wiring of my brain circuits and how they were stuck. What a relief to know I was not crazy!

Nonetheless, the stigma that characterizes many of the responses of people who do not understand mental health continues to challenge those with NVLD and others in the neurodiverse community.

Taking off the Mask

Until recently, our society largely rejected neurodivergent thinking and behaviors as normal. However, many NVLDers gain acceptance in the neurotypical world. People tend to overlook or downplay their differences in thinking and behavior because they respect the NVLD's stellar performance in their work environment or other areas. Those NVLDers who don't have skills high in demand or "desirable" talents have a much harder time fitting in and being respected.

As society gains awareness, it is my hope that those with neurodiversity will no longer need to mask their true selves. The first step is to acknowledge and validate the legitimacy of the difficulties and the emotional pain experienced by those with NVLD and other NDs. Healing and change cannot occur until the problem has been acknowledged.

Without treatment or a diagnosis, many NVLDers and NTs self-medicate with over-the-counter medication, alcohol, or illegal substances to minimize their pain and anxiety. If you are self-medicating, use the resources in this book to help yourself and seek professional help.

Lessons Learned

- The first step is acknowledging your difficulties and the resulting emotional pain.

- Identify the masks you wear and how they impact your relationships. Recognize that you may have co-occurring conditions, such as OCD, or may be misdiagnosed with those conditions because NVLD shares symptoms with them.

- Social skills training and development helps to minimize miscommunications and misinterpretations.

- Know the weak points in your decision-making process.

- Use the laws of large numbers and probability.

- Understand what exploitation is, and check with others to ascertain whether you are a victim.

- Learn about boundaries and include them in your skill set.

- Role-play with people you trust.

- Acknowledge your resilience and strengths during COVID while others struggle to adapt.

- When your child acts out, visualize them as a younger version of themselves to minimize your expectations of them. Focus on teaching them coping skills to manage their emotions instead of punishing them for their inappropriate behavior.

CHAPTER 8

Humpty Dumpty: Putting Yourself Together Again

> Humpty Dumpty sat on a wall,
> Humpty Dumpty had a great fall.
> All the King's horses
> And all the King's men
> Couldn't put Humpty together again.
> —English Nursery Rhyme

Not understanding why life was so difficult for me left me feeling broken and unsure of myself. I didn't know anyone who struggled as much as I did. It seemed like things were always so much harder for me, no matter what developmental stage I was in. Just like not being able to run away from your own shadow, these feelings of brokenness stayed with me throughout every experience. Like Humpty Dumpty, I felt helpless as to how to put all my shattered pieces back together.

The disparity between my difficulties and my strengths was so puzzling to me. How could I graduate college with honors and be so well-spoken yet get lost in buildings and have difficulty using keys to unlock doors, driving, learning, making friends, walking in a straight line, and communicating? In my young adult years, I was constantly underestimated by others. I have been told by many people that their first impression of me was that I was a "ditz," "space cadet," or "out to lunch." However, once they really got to know me, they were impressed with my intelligence and accomplishments.

Like most young people in their twenties, I wanted to be independent and make my own way in the world. However, since I often couldn't trust myself because of my inaccurate communication conclusions, I doubted my ability to make good decisions. I developed a pattern of behavior where I looked to others to approve of and validate me. I needed help to interpret the communication of others in my world. The problem was I needed too much help. Other than my family, I consumed too much of people's time, and they were overwhelmed by my needs. People could not comprehend the degree of my difficulties since I was so well-spoken. I wanted to be like others who lived on college campuses and went to parties. As time went on, I was so upset that others my age had moved on from college to jobs and moved away from home. I was in desperate need of help.

I went to so many therapists I lost count. Since I had a college degree and was articulate, the extent of my distress was overlooked. Most believed I viewed myself as a victim, exaggerated my circumstances, and took things too seriously (due to literal understanding of the words used to describe what was happening). The difficulties for which I needed help didn't align with those of my peers. Sometimes, I was seen as resistant when I showed little progress after their interventions.

Over the years, the system, which was supposed to help me, failed me and contributed to my emotional pain. At the time, like Humpty, I supposedly had the aid of the foremost experts, and I was still failing. The best counselors and therapists were those who were empathetic to my difficulties, and some of their suggestions were helpful but not enough to nearly scratch the surface.

I was frustrated and depressed that I couldn't create a functional, productive, and happy life. What could be so wrong with me that even with the help of professionals and trying my best, I still was not successful? You see, like Humpty Dumpty, no one was able to help me put the pieces back. It was hit or miss. No one could make sense of the symptoms or behaviors because they did not fit into any known diagnostic category. Now, fortunately, we have the NVLD Project, which has brought this little-known disorder to the attention of the public, professionals, and the editors of the *DSM*.

Putting Together the Pieces

Because I couldn't find a way, I was determined to make a way for my own benefit and that of others, just like the pioneers did to forge new territories. I had to become the explorer seeking interventions to help myself first and then my clients. My journey seems to be to help others experience less suffering than I did.

You, too, may feel like there are shattered and scattered pieces of yourself, and you may be struggling to put them back together to create a life for yourself. I will tell you what helped me and others with NVLD. Instead of taking the long and painful detours I did, you can take the most direct and efficient road to help yourself. Although there are many other treatment approaches and interventions, the ones I've chosen to include are, I believe, the most important ones to begin with.

Multimodal Approach

It can be overwhelming trying to put the pieces together with multiple professionals who may not all be on the same page. What has been most helpful to my clients is that I provide both remediation and a comprehensive intervention plan individualized to the client's unique needs. I am often asked to train professionals in other disciplines to help their own clients who may have NVLD.

A skilled conductor knows the exact moment to bring in each instrument to create a symphony of flowing music, just as a guide knows the treatment or intervention to bring in at each stage of the remediation process to help you to become the masterpiece that is *you*. It's important to work with professionals who are open, willing, supportive, and respectful of the work of all the various professionals and disciplines involved. Just like one instrument doesn't make the orchestra, one professional doesn't provide everything needed. This means the professionals involved must put aside their egos. If it takes one village to raise a neurotypical child, then it takes multiple villages to raise a neurodivergent child.

Starting Early

Finding the right type of help and support for each person and their particular challenges begins with early intervention. Once you see your child having difficulties with learning, cognitive functioning, social situations, or behaviors or showing signs of mental or emotional distress, it is time to intervene and get help. Avoiding the "wait and see" approach will give you much better outcomes. I can't tell you how many parents contact me during their children's middle school or young adult years looking for help.

Not realizing the ramifications, parents often tell themselves things such as "It will get better throughout the school year," or "My child needs a fresh start with a new teacher next year." Some wait until middle school when townships consolidate students from different schools, hoping their child will form friendships with kids who have no history with their children. If you're reading this book, hoping your child will improve, and have not sought help, I urge you to do so now.

Demystification and Self-Validation

It is important to learn about NVLD to set yourself free from the shame of self-blame and begin the process of self-validation. So, arm yourself with the knowledge in this book and the other resources that are available. Children can learn about NVLD at a level comparable to their age with increasing information as they get older. As part of the demystification process, it is necessary to understand the relationship between executive functioning, NVLD, and co-occurring conditions.

Executive Functioning (EF)

Housed in the brain's prefrontal cortex are the mind's executive functioning skills, which enable us to plan, prioritize, make decisions, regulate our emotions, and manage our behaviors. Thomas Brown, PhD, a clinical psychologist specializing in ADD/ADHD research and treatment, compares executive functioning (EF) to an orchestra. Even if each person in the orchestra is an outstanding musician, they need the conductor to guide them through the introduction of the woodwinds or the fading out of the strings and to convey the overall interpretation of the music to all players. Otherwise, the orchestra will sound terrible.

The Brain's Orchestra

Executive Functions	Abilities
Impulse Control	Thinking before speaking or acting, resisting temptation
Flexible Thinking	Creative problem-solving, adjusting to new situations, learning from mistakes, coping with routine changes, switching from one task to another
Emotional Control	Regulating emotions, choosing situation-appropriate emotional responses
Self-Monitoring	Self-awareness, adjusting actions and behaviors to suit the situation
Planning and Prioritizing	Planning daily tasks to meet short- and long-term goals
Task Initiation	Self-motivation, initiating tasks and directing actions
Organization	Managing and using belongings to efficiently complete tasks

Cognitive Processing Skills: The Foundation of Executive Functioning

Now imagine the conductor trying to create a symphony with broken or out-of-tune instruments. In such a situation, the quality and composition of the music would be compromised. The same is true for the mind's executive functioning system. Each "instrument," each cognitive processing skill, must function efficiently for optimal attention and learning to be achieved. When these cognitive mental processing skills are not fully developed, the brain's executive functioning skills system is impaired, and attention and learning are compromised. This causes difficulties in academic and social-emotional learning and self-management.

The Brain's Instruments: Cognitive Processing Skills

Skills	Abilities/Difficulties
Attention	Types: sustained, divided, and selective. Enables starting, staying on, and completing tasks
Long-Term Memory	Storing and recalling past learning / forgetting names and information studied for tests
Active Working Memory	Accessing information as needed while using it / remembering directions and steps in a process

Logic & Reasoning	Analysis and problem-solving
Auditory Processing	Recognizing and interpreting sounds / confusing similar words, decoding, reading comprehension, spelling, tuning out background noise, remembering what was said
Visual Processing	Comprehending and thinking in mental images / reading text, maps, charts, and graphs, spatial orientation, processing nonverbal communication
Processing Speed	Timely and accurate completion of work / receiving, understanding, and responding to incoming information / keeping up in school, work, social settings

EF Interventions

Although we have known about executive functioning skills for years, within the past ten years, educators, parents, and psychologists have recognized how important these skills are to academic and social-emotional learning, self-management, and behavior in general. In my experience, when schools and private practitioners work on improving these skills, parents and clients assume they use a comprehensive approach. However, despite widespread awareness of EF, what isn't discussed is the crucial role played by cognitive processing skills; these skills are the underlying foundation of the entire EF system. By and large, these services are really teaching individuals to compensate for their weaknesses instead of developing the underlying foundational (cognitive processing) skills that comprise the entire executive functioning system.

Compensatory Strategies

Compensatory strategies for poor executive functioning focus on developing the individual's strengths while employing strategies to cope with their weaknesses. These include reducing the homework load, preferential seating, untimed tests, structured scheduling, color coding, using timers, having a note-taker, voice-to-text writing, social problem-solving, and role-playing.

Although compensatory strategies can be helpful, poor EF skills are not outgrown and don't improve with age, despite learning how to cope with or manage them. These core skills must be fully developed so that individuals can function at an optimal level and be independent. Without appropriate interventions, the gap between NDs and NTs gets wider with each passing year. Ignoring these weaknesses by focusing on strengths, accommodations, and making modifications can be helpful, but it is not the whole answer. It's like wearing a brace around your ankle to assist with walking without undergoing physical therapy to make your ankle stronger.

Tutoring

Tutoring typically works well for students who have missed instructional time and need to catch up to the rest of the class. In most cases, tutoring is a short-term, temporary solution to catch up on content you have not yet learned because of an absence from the classroom. Unfortunately, many with NVLD and other learning disabilities who receive special education services, whether in public schools or private schools, have endured years of tutoring without becoming independent learners. It's a Band-Aid approach used for all ages and, at best, helps a person to get through school. Not only is tutoring often ineffective, but it can also be emotionally painful; the repeated frustrations and failures may create or contribute to anxiety, depression, low self-esteem, and lack of confidence.

Just 10 percent of learning problems stem from poor instruction, while 80 percent are the result of weak cognitive processing skills that can be enhanced with cognitive processing exercises, or "brain training." If your student needs repetitive reinforcement and instruction of curriculum material, with or without special education services, and is not intellectually impaired, then the cause of their struggles is most likely weak cognitive processing skills.

Tutoring can help; how and when it is used depends on individual circumstances. And compensatory strategies do offer ways to work around poor EF skills. But expecting individuals to develop the foundational EF mental processing skills necessary for optimal learning without strengthening cognitive processing skills is like going to the gas station for milk.

Neuroplasticity and Brain Training

Our brains are flexible and change through growth and reorganization. This process of change in response to experiences is known as neuroplasticity. When we learn, our brain makes new connections and forms new pathways.

Just like physical fitness can be improved by exercising the body, learning can be improved by exercising the cognitive skills of the mind. Strong cognitive processing skills make for easier and more efficient learning. Such brain training targets weak cognitive processing skills and develops them so that they become functional.

The training consists of repetitive mental exercises to create new neural connections and pathways in the brain made possible through neuroplasticity. Once the brain has made the changes, there is no going back, meaning the changes made will be lasting—much like driving, knitting, and other activities that can be done easily and almost effortlessly without conscious thinking and effort.

Ideally, after brain training, your cognitive processing skills will be functioning at optimal capacity, which will enable you to make the most progress in other areas of intervention. Just as a house needs a strong foundation to support itself, your mental processing needs to be strong to receive and apply the benefits from other therapies and interventions. Tutoring will now be much more effective with catching up and closing the gaps of material and concepts missed toward receiving grade-level instruction.

I continue to get feedback from children, and their parents, with whom I worked over the past twenty-five years, about how brain training changed their lives. While brain training is not a cure, it can significantly impact the quality of school life, relationships, and employment. A commitment of three to nine months is required for it to be effective. If you don't have a neuropsychological evaluation, a simple assessment of your cognitive processing skills is sufficient to determine if you are a candidate and what type of program(s) you need. Not all brain training programs are created equal, nor are all effective. So, before jumping in, do your own research to ensure that you are getting the training that will best meet your needs. For some suggestions, look at my website.

The evidence is accumulating that brain training is effective and long-lasting. But critics are quick to say there is no research or credible evidence to support the merits of brain training. I believe that, just as brain injury patients benefit from cognitive rehabilitation exercises that improve their executive function skills, people with NVLD and other learning disabilities can use the same type of exercises to build new neural pathways and improve their own executive functioning.

As I have said earlier in this book, you need help, and you need it now. Can you afford to wait another twenty years or more until more research is done to help yourself or a loved one? I would think not. I can wholeheartedly tell you, from my professional work, unless one is intellectually challenged, brain training can be a game-changer. Unlike Humpty, you will now be well on your way to putting together the pieces to success in other areas.

Social-Emotional Learning (SEL)

Since it's not just what you know but how you get along with others that determines life success, social skills interventions and training need to be a part of the process. Nonverbal communication deficits typically cause those with NVLD to have poor social skills.

Karl Albrecht is an executive management consultant, coach, futurist, lecturer, and author of more than twenty books on professional achievement, organizational performance, and business strategy. In his 2005 book, *Social Intelligence: The New Sign of Success*, he defines social intelligence as the ability to get along well with others and to get them to cooperate with you. According to Albrecht, that requires an understanding of social dynamics, self-insight, and awareness of how you perceive and react to what others do and say.

During my years of classroom teaching, I saw a lack of social skills in my students and a lack of social-emotional educational and training (SEL) programs. It broke my heart to see children not having any friends and being teased, excluded, and bullied, just like I was.

Those with NVLD desperately need to learn from their mistakes, make adjustments in their communication skills, and move forward. Learning social skills is imperative for mental health and well-being. Studies have shown that those with a network of friends and support are much happier and live longer than those lacking in this area. One of the reasons I left my tenured teaching position was to support social-emotional learning, as SEL intervention was not yet in the mainstream as it is today.

My work and experience with students have shown that poor executive functioning skills play a large part in social-emotional communication with others. What's often overlooked is the role EF functions, including auditory, visual, working memory, long-term memory, and processing speed play in processing verbal and nonverbal communication. When these skills are not functioning properly, it is harder to understand and remember what was said, keep up with the speed of conversations, and visually process body language. All of these skills work together to help people decipher incoming information that they need for effective social interactions. SEL programs are much more effective when these skills are intact.

A good social skills program teaches individuals to acquire and apply the knowledge, skills, and attitudes important for healthy self-concepts and social interactions. What I have found to be the most effective is to first teach these skills individually before progressing to group learning. Skills can be tailored to your child's daily interactions with their peers at school while in the classroom, during lunch and recess, and during after-school activities. Providing parents with a list of skills and activities is necessary to support and reinforce this learning at home.

Progress in social-emotional learning is enhanced through parent coaching during which parents learn how to speak in a way that makes sense to their children. In doing so, the NVLD child will be able to master these skills faster. Much like a coach, parents can hold practice sessions so their children will be better able to transfer these skills to their daily interactions with others. This better prepares them for group sessions, which are designed to reinforce what they have learned. Groups provide a safe setting where children can practice these newly learned skills.

Individuals who had social interventions as children may need continued support as adults as the demands are increased. Also, many adults did not have the benefits of social-emotional interventions because they were not diagnosed during their school years or such help was not available at that time. Adults can find many good resources online to help them learn social skills, individually or in groups.

Therapy

My experiences and those of others with NVLD have been that talk therapy *alone* is insufficient to meet the needs of children and adults with neurodivergent profiles, but it can be one part of the solution. Talk therapy, or psychotherapy, is a tool to identify and resolve issues that cause mental and emotional distress. While talk therapy can help us to cope with emotional suffering, it doesn't address neurodevelopmental skill deficits. One of the pitfalls of therapy for both children and adults with NVLD is when therapists inaccurately conclude their client's exceptional verbal intelligence and articulation are equal to all other areas of development. Verbal strengths often camouflage their developmental deficits.

By and large talk therapists are not trained in helping those whose brains work and see the world differently, let alone those with NVLD, as it's typically not addressed in their formal training. The focus needs to be on autonomy, rather than aspiring to be more like neurotypicals, while at the same time meeting their needs and balancing life in an NT world.

One of my clients has a therapist who encouraged her to use positive affirmations. Positive affirmations are ineffective for those who are unable to process nonverbal communication and the issues surrounding them. Telling yourself, "I communicate easily and effectively," is not going to be helpful. This experience left her feeling invalidated and misunderstood; affirmations had done nothing to help her develop the skills she desperately needed.

A former client told her therapist that her husband was upset by the disarray in her closet, the marks on the walls he had to repaint because of her banging into them with objects, and her carelessness when cooking. Her therapist responded by telling her she needed to be more mindful and respectful of her husband's needs. Despite the therapist knowing that her client had NVLD, she didn't grasp that her difficulties were due to poor visual-spatial and executive functioning skills. My client felt so ashamed and rejected by her therapist that she ended therapy. The appropriate response was to validate her struggles and then help her to improve in these areas.

As an NVLD specialist, I approached this situation from a skill-building model. First, I addressed her feelings of shame and inadequacy and then affirmed that her behavior was not disrespectful to her husband. Next, I gave her husband some resources to help him learn more about NVLD. Once he understood that his wife's developmental skills were not equal in all areas, he was able to work with her instead of against her. We came up with "zones" in their home that he agreed would be out of his jurisdiction to complain about. Now, when she leaves marks on the walls due to her poor visual-spatial deficits, he lovingly refers to her as his "bull in a china shop" as he touches them up with paint. She now has strategies she uses when cooking to reduce the mess she makes. She also has a checklist to make sure she has cleaned up efficiently.

Most therapists are not trained to help clients manage NVLD or other learning disabilities. They do not understand how a learning disability diagnosis differs from neurotypical diagnoses. There is a great deal of overlap between neurodivergent disorders and mental health issues. While traditional therapy methods may be effective with NTs, they do not always work for NDs.

When misdiagnosis and misunderstanding are part of the therapeutic process, it can add to a person's anguish and exacerbate their struggles with their already fragile emotional health and mental well-being. Some therapists may not understand the need of those with NVLD to ask lots of questions to compensate for their lack of understanding and interpret this behavior as noncompliance in the therapeutic process. These individuals may have been misdiagnosed with borderline personality disorder and oppositional defiant disorder because of the crossover of symptoms, meltdowns, and behavioral reactions. Misdiagnosed children will have no idea that the treatment they are receiving does not match their needs, further compounding their challenges.

Dialectical Behavioral Therapy (DBT)

DBT can be more helpful than the more traditional cognitive behavioral therapy (CBT) since it focuses on helping individuals to *apply* the skills to specific challenges and events in their lives. The main goals of DBT are to teach people how to live in the moment through mindfulness training, develop healthy ways to cope with stress, regulate their emotions, and improve their relationships with others. Although designed for those with borderline personality disorder, it can help those with NVLD and other chronic disorders. I have tailored the foundational skills portion of DBT for inclusion within my interventions to meet the needs of my clients. In my professional experience, the cognitive processing and EF skills, which are the foundation of social-emotional learning (SEL), must be strengthened before skills learned in DBT can be effectively applied and implemented.

Although DBT isn't a replacement for social-emotional learning, it teaches how to manage the stress of living with NVLD. I have worked with parents and adults who have raved about DBT and others who have tried it and had few to no results or about the same as regular talk therapy. The following feedback is based on my professional experiences and client feedback.

Pros of DBT

- It is structured.
- It is skill-based (emotional, mindfulness, distress tolerance, interpersonal).
- It offers individual and group skills sessions.
- It decreases the likelihood of acting on suicidal ideation.

- There is ten-minute coaching support in between scheduled sessions for situational issues.
- It promotes goal setting.
- It focuses on leading to a productive life.

Cons of DBT

- It can be very expensive.
- Some practitioners require intensive and consistent family involvement (individual, parent, joint, and group sessions) in treatment. Many participants have reported little success with the large number of sessions they must attend, and few can afford the cost.
- Skills can be difficult to apply in the moment as needed.
- The curriculum is fast-paced and time-limited; many NVLDers do not have enough time to process the skills before moving to the next topic.
- It requires tasks that are difficult for people with executive functioning deficits unless they have been modified by a therapist who understands the client's struggles.
- It can be too rigid when it isn't tailored to the needs of those with NVLD.
- Participants need to be able to self-motivate and initiate tasks.
- Most DBT therapists are resistant to combining DBT with other therapeutic modalities and frequently dismiss cognitive therapeutic approaches, like executive functioning skills exercises, as ineffective.

- Although troubleshooting is a big part of the DBT approach, many DBT therapists are not available for real-time help.
- It is not a treatment for trauma, as the focus is distracting oneself into other activities.

Finding the Right Therapist: They're Out There!

A good therapist can be an important part of the NVLDer's support system when they understand their unique neurodevelopmental profile. Finding the right therapist is not an easy task. As an NVLD advocate, I feel it's important for the NVLD consumer population to know that many therapists may not have the background, experience, or training to help them, which is a consequence of it not being an official *DSM* disorder. In my personal experience, some therapists can also be damaging and invalidating when they misunderstand NVLD, and their clients will need more therapy to undo the impact of the therapist's efforts. I recommend that any therapist you hire have significant life experience to balance their theoretical approaches and suggest you see someone with fifteen or more years of experience.

As it becomes more recognized, be mindful that anyone can say they know about NVLD and add it to the list of disorders they treat. If a therapist says they have experience working with NVLD, be sure to ask them if they know the impaired developmental areas of the disorder, its symptoms, and specific examples of the issues their clients have faced and how they have helped them.

Some therapists may say they are not familiar with NVLD but would still be willing to work with you. You may then ask them if they would do the necessary research to learn about NVLD. Good therapists will take it upon themselves to review the research and the resources provided by the NVLD Project. Or you may want to give them this book to read, which will help them better understand you and assist you with implementing some of the recommendations. You do not want to find yourself educating your therapist during valuable session times that cost you money!

If the therapist agrees, ask them to contact you, after doing their research, to discuss if they think they can help you. If you feel this therapist could be a good fit for you, go ahead and schedule an appointment. If you have a good rapport with the therapist, you can arrange to continue once a week, on a month-to-month basis, to see if the therapy is helping you to cope with the daily challenges of living with NVLD.

If you need help finding a therapist, ask a friend, teacher, or family member. This is a helpful way to find out the names of people others have liked working with, but that does not guarantee you will have that same experience. Of course, it goes without saying that, as in all professions, there is a wide range of expertise, competency, and rapport. It's your job as a consumer to keep looking until you find the person who is right for you. Having a therapist who can meet your needs is an invaluable asset and will greatly contribute to your success.

Real-Time Assistance

Keep in mind that having a session once a week for one hour with a professional may not be enough to meet your needs. Wondering whether you are understanding a real-life situation correctly can be stressful, but by the time you get to your therapy appointment, your ability to effectively respond to the situation may have passed. The resulting anxiety often leads the NVLDers to overreact, which may then damage their relationships and increase their depression and despair.

You need someone from your support network you can call or text to check things out as they occur in the moment, such as a conflict with a friend, a job offer, or any situation that you are not sure how to approach. Real-time assistance gives you the skills and support you need. Look back at the examples of real-life situations in the preceding chapters to see how having access to real-time assistance would have made a difference in the outcome. Real-time assistance is also beneficial for children to help them implement and improve their interactions with peers and in other situations and relationships.

How I Built My Village

My first source of support outside my family was Rob, whom I met just as I started college and later married. He saw both my strengths and my struggles and provided me with twenty-four/seven support because he believed I would be successful and a good life partner. Though I felt only capable of obtaining an associate's degree, Rob pushed me to earn a bachelor's degree. I graduated with honors and went on to receive my master's degree.

Rob's support helped me build the confidence to seek others who could help me. I had the great good fortune to meet a therapist who understood me in a way a score of therapists had not. She validated my initial research on NVLD and how I experienced it myself. As we navigated this unchartered territory together, her affirmation inspired me to create a life worth living.

Looking back, I realize it was those people who encouraged me to keep going on those days when I could not get out of bed, when I couldn't see the road ahead or my life's purpose. Their belief in me ignited my burning desire to help others avoid the pain and hardships I had been through.

My village continued to fan those flames as I set about to fulfill my mission by teaching and starting my own business. That encouragement enabled me to find innovative ways to help myself and eventually others with NVLD, ADHD, learning disabilities, and some on the spectrum as well. Today, my village includes other professionals, new friends, and, most important, my clients. Their progress is my inspiration. Like the Olympics' eternal flame, my fire still blazes with the same intensity as it did all those years ago.

It Takes a Whole Village

The Nigerian proverb "It takes a whole village to raise a child" exists in different forms in many African languages. The basic meaning is that a child's upbringing is a communal effort. Whether you are the person providing support for your child or spouse or an adult coping with NVLD, you'll need to put together your own village of support. This entails engaging people with different skill sets, as it's not possible for one person to meet all of your needs.

Those with NVLD need guidance and validation from others to make sense of things. In addition to the skill development professionals within your village, there are those guides, mentors, and friends who can support your overall sense of self and well-being by just being present for you. I was very fortunate to have had someone, in addition to my father, who gave me the gift of presence. When you are truly seen and recognized for who you are, you have the foundation to begin to build the confidence to move forward.

When someone is present for you (also known as "holding space"), they put their own needs aside to provide a safe, supportive, nurturing, nonjudgmental environment to listen to you and validate your authentic self. In other words, the time spent with them isn't about them. It's about them being there for you, in complete acceptance of your experiences, trying to see things from your perspective, without any attempts to change the way you feel. It's important that when you do have such a person in your life, you don't take them for granted. Find a way to acknowledge how much you appreciate their support with expressions of gratitude, such as movie dates or sending cards or doing favors in return.

How do you begin to assemble your network of guides, mentors, friends, and clergy, among others? It takes perseverance and creativity. They may appear naturally and informally through the relationships you develop in various environments, or you may need to formally ask someone who is trustworthy and objective to help you. You can start out looking to your immediate family members who are open to being there for you or who already are. If you have grandparents, include them, as they usually have more time and most likely want to help you. You can give them this book to learn more about the neurodiverse population. Your family's presence can be a comfort to you, even if it's just spending time together making a meal or watching a movie. A close friend you can spend time with who enjoys your company can also be a resource for you.

Even though you may be tempted to stay within yourself, putting yourself in environments where you will meet other people is important. Join an activity where you see the same people regularly. Take your time, and be careful not to overshare. Let these relationships develop at a slow pace. You may find one person you have a good rapport with to include in your support network.

Internships or volunteer opportunities that provide you with mentors can be another resource. Mentors are open to sharing their experiences and knowledge to guide you. Mentor relationships can also develop into personal relationships. If so inclined, you can join a church. If this isn't your thing, try Unitarian churches or branches of the Ethical Culture Society that are open to people from all walks of life regardless of their beliefs.

It is important to remember that although you may feel broken, you are not. You were born perfectly whole in a world that demands conformity to the thinking and ways of the majority neurotypical population. Back in Humpty's day, he didn't have the glue to put himself back together. We are fortunate to have neuroscientific research, specialized learning programs, online support groups, and the NVLD Project to help us help ourselves become whole.

Lessons Learned

- Avoid the wait-and-see approach for better, more optimal outcomes.
- It's never too late to help yourself.
- Build your village.
- Using research, educate yourself about NVLD and executive functioning.
- Neuroplasticity and brain training make it possible to significantly increase your level of functioning.
- Understand the role NVLD plays at home, in school, in relationships, and on the job.
- Shop for a therapist to find one who understands NVLD and is a good fit for you in terms of personality and skill level.
- Engage in social-emotional learning.
- Use a "conductor" to manage your treatment plan with multidisciplinary professionals.
- Identify people in your village and your professional network who can provide you with real-time assistance at the moment you need it.
- Be aware of scams and unrealistic promises.

Chapter 9

Mind, Body, Spirit: Healing Your Whole Self

Doing versus Being

Whether you're working with a child or an adult or trying to help yourself, the connection to your "self" or spirit isn't just all about what you do to improve on your weaknesses; it's also about embracing your authentic self so that you can be who you truly are. This happens when you lovingly take care of yourself by nurturing your mind, body, and spirit.

I hope that by sharing the story of my healing, along with some holistic therapeutic approaches, I can help you find the inspiration and tools to nurture your whole self. My path is meant to show you what is possible. There are many paths to putting yourself back together again. Choose the ones that feel right for you.

My Healing

Many years ago, I was so physically sick I could barely function, and at the same time, I was fighting a severe battle with depression from the impact of living with NVLD. The stress of having NVLD but not being able to manage all of the symptoms contributed to a huge, daily release of cortisol into my nervous system, which impaired my immune system's functioning.

The conventional doctors I saw were unable to help me. None of them could accurately identify the cause of my illness or provide any effective treatment. The medications I took did little or nothing to help me, while their side effects exacerbated my overall feeling of extreme illness. Every day, I experienced hours of headache and crushing fatigue that made it difficult for me to walk across the room. It was a struggle to get through my workday, and once I got home again, I immediately crashed on the sofa and slept until the next morning. Attempting to eat well was difficult; it was too hard to get from the couch to the kitchen to even peel a vegetable.

One day, when I was feeling worse than usual, I asked God to help me. I had no idea where else to turn or what else I could do. I asked him to please send me help or a sign letting me know he was listening. The next day, I stumbled upon a holistic practitioner who ultimately helped me to not only get better but to get my life back. I was skeptical, and rightly so, since this was not the traditional medical route. I doubted that diet, nutrition, supplementation, and energy psychology could help. But it didn't seem like it would hurt either, so I worked with this practitioner twice a week for almost two years. My emotional and physical health improved through my work with holistic practitioners and my renewed interest in living a healthier life.

Gut-Brain Connection and Nutrition

Nutrition has been a game-changer for many of the people I have worked with over the years. It's no secret that we are what we eat. Movies like *Fed Up*, *Forks over Knives*, and *Heal* have made it apparent that good nutrition is essential to our mental and physical health. The stomach, connected to the brain by the vagus nerve, is considered to be the "second brain." What we eat can cause or contribute to anxiety and depression, particularly for people who are gluten-sensitive or have celiac disease.

Gluten

Gluten is a protein found in wheat, rye, barley, processed foods, and certain toiletry items. It is also used as a binding agent, like glue, to hold food together by giving it a greater consistency. Gluten sensitivity and celiac disease have similar symptoms and are not easily distinguished. Both can cause irritability, depression, anxiety, attention and learning deficits, and digestive problems. For people with celiac disease, the effects are longer-term. Standard lab tests may not reveal that you have one of these conditions.

The best way to determine whether gluten poses health issues for you is to eliminate it from your diet. Try an experiment: remove foods containing gluten for fourteen days and see how you feel.

When I did this, both my digestive issues and depression significantly improved. I was no longer irritable and was better able to focus. Each time I accidentally ate gluten, I felt depressed and anxious. Becoming gluten-free was crucial for my emotional well-being and changed my life.

Supplements

Like many people, I had no idea that vitamins and minerals are key contributors to our mental health. Being deficient in just one nutrient can negatively impact the functioning of your body and brain. Our bodies produce the hormones cortisol and adrenaline as a protective mechanism against stress. Reacting to stress over a long period of time causes the adrenal glands to burn out, resulting in adrenal fatigue and compromising the immune system. I now know that my health problems were triggered by the ongoing emotional stress of living with NVLD.

Supplements provide nutrients we don't get from eating overly processed foods. They can also help us to better absorb the nutrients from food. It stands to reason that if NVLD is a brain-based disorder, we need to keep our brains in the best possible shape. I try to take my supplements every morning; when I forget, my family and friends often notice the difference in my mood and behavior and remind me to take them. I don't like swallowing pills, so I open the capsules and pour the granules into my morning smoothie. This works well for children who have difficulty swallowing pills.

Before taking supplements, always consult with your doctor. They may have side effects or negatively interact with prescription drugs. In my experience, organic and non-GMO supplements sourced in the United States and verified by independent labs produce the best results. You can identify these by looking for a USP (*United States Pharmacopeia)* verified mark on the packaging.

Energy Psychology and Holistic Therapeutic Approaches

A basic premise of holistic health theory is that emotional memories remain in the mind and body. Earlier I talked about the work of William W. Dodson, who studied the impact of the twenty thousand additional negative messages people with ADHD receive every day.

When painful emotions are not processed and released, they can create or contribute to the dysregulation, depression, anxiety, and physical illness seen in those with neurodivergent disorders.

Since ancient times, cultures around the globe have embraced the idea that an unseen energy flows through all living things and is connected directly to health. The existence of this life force energy has been verified by recent scientific experiments, and medical professionals are becoming increasingly aware of its role in the functioning of the immune system and the healing process.

Energy psychology is based on Einstein's theory that all material objects, including the human body, consist of energy and generate electromagnetic fields. This life force of energy flows within the physical body through pathways called *chakras*, *meridians*, and *nadirs* as well as around our bodies in auras.

This life force energy nourishes the organs and cells of the body, supporting their vital functions, and is responsive to thoughts and feelings. It becomes disrupted when we accept, either consciously or unconsciously, negative thoughts or feelings about ourselves. At that point, one or more organs of the body may cease to function normally.

Energy psychology (EP) is becoming more recognized as a credible treatment practice, much like chiropractors were once considered quacks and are now covered by health insurance. EP incorporates a variety of treatment approaches that stimulate organs to rapidly release deep-seated, traumatic emotions in a way that talk therapy cannot. EP applications clear emotional blockages in and around the physical body by correcting energetic imbalances. This improves the flow of energy in the body's electromagnetic field, which supports and restores physical, emotional, and spiritual well-being.

EP can be done alone or with a practitioner. According to the Association for Comprehensive Energy Psychology, EP meets the criteria for evidenced-based treatment. However, it is recommended that these interventions be adjuncts to an integrative therapeutic approach. They are not meant as a replacement for medical or psychological treatment.

Reiki

Reiki, which originated in Japan, is a time-honored method that reduces stress, eases pain, balances emotions, enhances mental clarity, and facilitates personal and spiritual growth. Reiki heals by flowing through the affected parts of the energy field and charging them with positive energy. It raises the vibratory level of the energy field in and around the physical body, causing the negative energy to break apart and fall away. In so doing, Reiki clears, strengthens, and heals the energy pathways to create feelings of peace and harmony. Reiki is now accepted and offered in many hospitals, hospices, spas, and wellness centers.

At one point in my life, I had Reiki sessions twice a week for two years. They contributed greatly to my well-being, and I continue to participate in sessions when needed. I recommend trying reiki on a weekly basis. If this is costly, try doing a few sessions for the experience, and then you can follow up by taking a class to learn how to do it for yourself.

Emotional Freedom Technique (EFT)

EFT, also known as "tapping," is a self-help method that stimulates acupuncture points on the body. Using your fingertips, you apply pressure to energy meridians while verbally making statements about an issue that you want to resolve. It's one way to get unstuck and restore balance to your body's energy system. EFT has benefits as a treatment for anxiety, depression, physical pain, and insomnia. You can download a free tapping manual online at EFT International.

Eye Movement Desensitization and Reprocessing (EMDR)

We all replay upsetting thoughts and experiences, wondering what we could have done or said differently to reduce the painful outcome or our response to it. I have worked with many adults who continue to carry pain, shame, and self-blame for the abuse they suffered by teachers, peers who bullied them, and parents who did not understand them. They continue to feel insecure and unworthy.

EMDR is a type of psychotherapy that helps people heal from the psychological trauma caused by disturbing life experiences, such as the trauma sustained by war veterans and the trauma inflicted on domestic violence victims and sexually abused children. It typically takes years for the mind to recover with other forms of therapy; with EMDR, healing can occur much faster.

During a treatment, a trained therapist asks the client to recall painful memories as the therapist guides them to make specific eye movements to transform the meaning of the traumatic events on an emotional level. EMDR, which is covered by most insurance companies, has helped individuals struggling with trauma, anxiety, depression, and panic disorders. It is recognized as an effective form of treatment by many national and international organizations.

Meditation

Meditation is simply a way of relaxing and expanding your awareness to achieve a calm emotional state. If you are anything like me, the word meditation may make you cringe. There are many things I would rather do with my time than try to sit quietly and block out the constant chatter in my mind, especially since I have ADHD. This is precisely why you need to find a meditation practice that is fun and fulfilling and will help you to dial down unproductive bombarding thoughts.

There are many different types of meditation, including mindfulness, loving-kindness, Zen, and mantra. It doesn't need to be elaborate; you can do something as simple as focusing on your breath, going for a walk, looking at the sunset, or listening to the waves of the ocean. I personally like using guided meditation apps, as they complement my style of thinking. YouTube has so many meditation videos that you're bound to find some that work for you.

Breath Work

Breathing acts as a bridge between spirit, mind, and body, between the conscious and the subconscious, according to the International Breathwork Foundation. An umbrella term that describes a wide range of conscious breathing practices, *breath work* promotes awareness, self-regulation, and deep personal transformation. The goal is to enhance inner peace, health, and well-being. There are many different types of breath work exercises that are simple enough to do. I highly recommend trying Wim Hof's method, which you can access on YouTube or by downloading his free app.

Self-Compassion

We need to treat ourselves with the same compassion we show others who are suffering. That means treating yourself with warmth and understanding when you are having a difficult time, struggling with an important task, or notice something you don't like about yourself. How many times a day do you beat yourself up for not doing something right? Are you able to drop the self-judgment when you misunderstand what someone has said?

Ask yourself this: Has beating yourself up, calling yourself names, and putting yourself down ever made you feel better about yourself? Would you berate your friend or loved one the same way you do yourself? Would you condemn a blind person for bumping into you, a paralyzed person for needing assistance, a homeless person for being hungry, a sick person for resting? Of course not!

Part of practicing self-compassion is acknowledging, in the moment when you may feel misunderstood, foolish, or judged by others, that their comments are not about your lack of intelligence or ability but about the way you process nonverbal communication information. In these situations, hold your head up high, take a deep breath, and confidently state you need some more clarification because your brain works differently sometimes. How we respond and treat ourselves teaches others how we expect to be treated.

The next time you put yourself down for struggling or making a mistake, ask yourself what you would say to someone else in the same situation. That is exactly what you need to be saying to yourself! Instead of beating yourself up, acknowledge your feelings.

Learn more about Dr. Kristen Neff's approach to developing self-compassion and how to access her free exercises and meditations in my resource section.

Faith and Prayer

Faith and spirituality have been important pieces of my support system. While some people identify with a type of religion, others believe in a higher power, God, angels, the universe, or a combination of these. Although this isn't a book about religion, I encourage you to find faith in something that resonates with and supports you. Prayer and faith can elicit feelings of gratitude, compassion, forgiveness, and hope, which are associated with healing and wellness.

The Ho'oponopono Prayer can be really effective when you're feeling frustrated or angry at the neurotypical world and wishing, as many have described it to me, that you'd never been cursed with NVLD. It's an ancient Hawaiian ritual for reconciliation, understanding, kindness, and forgiveness. Ho'oponopono means to "cause things to move back in balance" or to "make things right"—to have compassion for others and yourself.

The prayer goes as follows:

"I'm sorry. Please forgive me. Thank you. I love you."

Repetition of this self-love mantra enables you to release challenging emotions and move on. You can play the prayer on YouTube or record it and listen to it on your phone as you move throughout your day. It's also helpful to write the four statements on sticky notes and put them in places around your home where you will see them and remember to say them out loud or to yourself. Soon, you will be saying them automatically with little or no intentional thought.

Gratitude

My dad taught me the importance of being grateful, but as my challenges increased from childhood to adulthood, my practice fell to the wayside. It was hard to be grateful for what I had when I was suffering. I looked for studies that verified the power of gratitude and discovered that, in fact, it has been demonstrated to increase happiness. In 2016, researchers at Indiana University found that practicing gratitude by journaling about the positive things in their lives improved the mental health of both people in therapy and people not in therapy.

I began to practice gratitude exercises without any expectations. Gradually, I developed a more positive attitude by focusing on what I was grateful for rather than on what I was unsatisfied with in my life. As a result, I started to feel happier.

While it's certainly not a cure for NVLD, gratitude can help. It's important to remember that gratitude is an ongoing process. It's easy to do when things are going well but not so easy when you are faced with challenges. Regardless of your circumstances, try being grateful for what you have, and you will attract more experiences and resources in your life for which to be grateful.

Sound Therapy

Have you ever listened to a song that made you feel encouraged or on top of the world? Most of us know the feeling of driving down the road on a bright, beautiful day with the windows down while singing along to our favorites. Isn't it a great feeling? Music is a universal language that can change the way we feel.

David M. Greenberg, a music psychologist, says tracks to get you out of bed should begin gently and slowly, such as Coldplay's "Viva La Vida" and "Lovely Day" by Bill Withers. Songs like these have predictable beginnings, middles, and endings, which makes it easier to finish the corresponding task and transition to the next activity.

I love using music to alter my mood and have created "music menus" consisting of various playlists to relax, exercise, focus, and help get started with mundane tasks. Try making playlists for yourself or your child. Playlists can guide you through a sequence of steps within a routine task or the transition from one task to another—both of which may be difficult for those with NVLD, ADHD, and autism. Each activity should correspond to a song on the playlist in the order it needs to be completed. Use songs that are approximately three to four minutes long so each song can be used as a timer. Select songs with tempos that are appropriate to the tasks, have positive and encouraging lyrics, and are enjoyable.

The Listening Program (TLP)

TLP is a research-based music listening therapy program for achieving optimum brain health and functioning, which helps those with NVLD and NDs with executive functioning, anxiety, focus, and academics. As a certified practitioner of the TLP by Advanced Brain Technologies, I have helped many using this program. To learn more about it, go here: https://advancedbrain.com. If you choose to purchase the program, be sure to use my code ALC for a discount on the equipment

Essential Oils (EO) and Aromatherapy

The use of essential oils to enhance well-being dates back to 4500 BC. These oils can be used for focus, sleep, motivation, and relaxation. Essential oils (EO) are compounds extracted from plants (trees, bushes, seeds, roots, flowers) that contain the plants' unique scent. They are applied to the temples, wrists, and behind the ears or diffused in a room.

EO is a daily part of my life. I use them when I wake up, while working, and at bedtime. Match the various types of oils to your individual needs—motivation, focus, learning, relaxing, transitioning. Vetiver is the best oil for focus and helps to calm emotions. Lavender aids sleep. To be effective, essential oils must be 100 percent plant-based, free of synthetics and fillers, and quality-controlled. You can learn more about essential oils from the National Association for Holistic Aromatherapy.

Medication

Although holistic modalities are included in this book, I do not want to give the impression that they are a means to an end. Some physical and mental conditions can be improved without medication by changing diet, exercising, supplementation and so on. Some of these things are common sense and can improve one's condition generally, but even so it may not be enough and varies per person.

At this time (August 2022), there is no medication that effectively addresses symptoms of NVLD. However, many people who have NVLD have been misdiagnosed with ADHD and prescribed a medication designed for ADHD symptoms.

Finding the right medication for a specific individual with ADHD almost always requires the individual to try medications one by one until one of them is found to be effective. When someone with NVLD is misdiagnosed with ADHD, they will not only go through several medication trials but also likely suffer adverse side effects from at least some of the medications. In the best-case scenario, the doctor will conclude that the patient is nonresponsive to ADHD medication and discontinue prescribing ADHD medications. Many people will continue on medication that is doing little to nothing to help them, which may lead to other complications.

Some people with NVLD may need medication for symptoms caused by the emotional strain of NVLD (such as anxiety or depression). People with NVLD can experience mild, moderate or severe NVLD symptoms at any time as well as co-occurring disorders that can helped with medication.

There are many different opinions about psychotropic medications in our society.

It's regrettable that the stigma around taking medication for invisible mental and emotional difficulties prevents many people from feeling better. Medication is viewed by most of the public as fine for physical maladies, but as "a crutch" for people with brain-based disorders and mental health issues. Many of the parents and adults coping with NVLD, ADHD, and other disorders I have worked with over the years initially refused to consider medication to avoid "drugging" themselves or their child. Yet often, after exhausting every possible alternative, the choice to take medications comes down to preserving quality of life for you and your child. When life is difficult, many conclude that the potential risks and side effects of medication are better than the downward spiral on the horizon. At this point, I think trying medication is worth the possibility that they will greatly benefit the NVLDer, and in some instances, maybe even save their life.

Taking medication is a personal decision. I encourage you to seek out a highly trained psychiatrist or psychopharmacologist with whom to discuss your options.

Recovery International (RI)

Recovery is a free national nonprofit organization that helps people to cope with depression and anxiety. I recommend this organization to my clients. Their program gives people the tools to identify and combat negative feelings regardless of the cause of their distress. Developed by a neuropsychiatrist, this peer-led self-help model, based on cognitive-behavioral training, gives you a safe space to cope with the difficulties you are facing. Peer mentors can provide real-time support, much like having a sponsor in AA (alcoholics anonymous) to help practice the tools of the program between group-led meetings.

You can learn how to take responsibility for your well-being, confront learned helplessness, identify and manage negative thoughts, feelings, beliefs, and behaviors that can lead to emotional distress and related physical symptoms. Visit RI's website for resources and meetings near you.

Multimodality Therapy

There are many other types of energy psychology, holistic healing methods and other more traditional modalities—too many to list within the scope of this book. In my experience, optimal progress occurs when there is a combination of more than one method of treatment. By making improvements in each area of treatment, you get the advantage of each modality which adds up to overall gains. Some modalities can be done at the same time while others can be incorporated when the previous treatment is completed. Now that you have a better understanding of the connection between mind, body, and spirit and the available resources, you can discover what works for you and add it to your repertoire of coping mechanisms. Be sure to consult with your doctor first before implementing any changes in your health-care routine.

Your Mindset

We are all shaped by our experiences and our thoughts about ourselves. The pain experienced by some people with NVLD is heartbreaking. To have happy, fulfilling lives, we must make peace with NVLD and begin to positively change our mindsets by taking charge of our thoughts and actions. The choice is yours, and only you can make it.

At their annual live seminar, Think Better, Live Better, Marc and Angel Chernoff guide attendees through this process of perspective change. Inner peace begins whenever you take a new breath and choose not to allow other people or some uncontrollable event to affect your happiness and well-being. You are not what they say about you. You are not what happened to you. You are what you choose to become at this moment. Let go, breathe, and begin. For more from the Chernoffs on changing your mindset, visit www.marcandangel.com

Let Go, Breathe, and Begin
Written by Mark and Angel Chernoff

Today, remind yourself that you have spent too much of your life thinking too little of yourself. You tried to become smaller. Quieter. Less sensitive. Less opinionated. Less needy. Less *you*. You felt broken, and you didn't want to be too much or push people away. You wanted to fit in. You wanted people to like you. You wanted to make a good impression. You wanted to be wanted. So, you could feel healed.

And so, for years, you talked down to yourself, and sacrificed your peace of mind for the sake of making other people happy.

And for years, you suffered.

But you're tired of suffering, and you're done thinking you aren't good enough just the way you are. Right? Good!

It's not your job to change who you are in order to become someone else's idea of a worthwhile human being. You are worthwhile. Not because other people think you are, but because you are breathing your own air, and therefore you matter. Your truth matters. Your feelings matter. Your voice matters. And with or without anyone's approval or permission, you must be who you are and live your truth. Even if it makes people turn their heads. Even if it makes them uncomfortable. Even if they choose to leave.

Even if your own confidence in yourself has been shaken!

The real battle is in your mind. And your mind is under your control, not the other way around. You may have been broken down by adversity or rejection or stress, but *you* are not broken. So, don't let others convince you otherwise. And don't let your mind get the best of you either.

Heal yourself by refusing to belittle yourself. Choose to take up a lot of positive space in your own life today. Choose to give yourself permission to meet your own needs. Choose to honor your feelings and emotions. Choose to make self-love and self-care your priorities.

Choose to think better about yourself, so you can live better in spite of the circumstances you face.

Lessons Learned

- Pay attention to your thoughts and actions to actively replace negatives with positives and change your mindset.
- Do not let your struggles with NVLD define you—embrace your talents, interests, assets, and goals to nurture your authentic self.
- Practice self-care using techniques such as energy psychology, self-compassion, EMDR, Reiki, massage, essential oils, breathing exercises, gratitude, and meditation.
- Regular exercise, a healthy diet, and vitamin and mineral supplements will help you feel your best.
- Improve your executive functioning through sound therapy and brain training.
- Seek out a highly trained psychiatrist or psychopharmacologist with whom to discuss your options.

Chapter 10

Telling It Like It Is: Everyday NVLD

Raising a child with NVLD is much different than rearing a neurotypical child. Parents, the sooner you understand and look beyond their behavior to see your child's needs, replace your criticism with compassion, and provide them with every kind of support they need, the sooner your child can begin to thrive instead of hide. View the school system as your ally, not your adversary, and exhaust all options it can provide you before taking other measures. If homeschooling your child is a viable option, there are tutors and online programs to fill in the gaps for the unfamiliar subject matter. It might not be easy, but remember, it may be necessary for your child's well-being, which is more important than academics.

Set up your home to encourage your child's success and independence. There are resources, some of which I have mentioned in this book, to help you with strategies at home and in your daily activities, including providing structure, scheduling, making checklists, managing transitions, completing, homework, enforcing rules, providing rewards and consequences, and more. What I see in my work with parents isn't a lack of knowledge but rather questions about how to utilize, apply, and implement it. Most parents will need training to equip themselves with the skills they need to help their children achieve the goals of self-sufficiency and independence. Obtain training from a professional who will create a plan tailored to your child's needs and follow through.

Much like your child, you, too, will need real-time assistance for those tough moments when you're alone, challenged, and overwhelmed. While talking about your feelings and frustration with a therapist is good for the short term, it's not enough to achieve this long-term goal. That requires engineering a structured and supportive environment. Use real-time assistance (phone calls, texts) until you have enough experience to go it alone. Parents will also have more success applying the strategies if children participate in cognitive brain training to improve executive functioning and increase self-esteem and confidence.

Instill in your child a "find a way" attitude while also fostering an understanding and acceptance regarding the things that are hard for them. This is a balance between understanding and empathizing and focusing on skill development, expectations, responsibility, and accountability. Many parents overidentify with the difficulties faced by their children and, as a result, feel bad watching them struggle. NVLD is an explanation, not an excuse to absolve your child of responsibility. When parents are unable to confront their discomfort and hold their children accountable, the consequences are high.

Tough Love

Holding your child accountable for their behavior (with support in place) is hard work, and although it may be easier to give in at that moment, in the long run, you are not helping your child or yourself. Children who are not held accountable often become demanding and needy adults with little resilience or resources to help themselves. These adult children may end up "running the household" while the parents do the caretaking. It is much harder to start this process with an adult child in a big body, especially if they don't want help or have the awareness to know they need help. The rigid and inflexible thinking of the NVLDer is often the underlying reason why some lack insight. Pushback behaviors are hard to manage at this stage of the game, which is why starting early is imperative.

Unfortunately, it may be necessary for you to apply a tough-love approach depending upon the severity of the situation. Sometimes these young adults can create so much havoc at home that keeping them there is no longer an option. Some individuals need to experience the consequences of their actions to gain the self-awareness needed to be open to receiving help. Many parents struggle with this, as they want to protect their children and keep them out of trouble. However, you can't do this forever. If you have reached this point, the only way out may be to let them go and reap the consequences of their behaviors until they are willing to make changes.

Caretaking and Holding Space

Regardless of their age, your child will need the help of many different people. The bulk of the caretaking often comes under the heading of "mothering" because women, more often than not, are the ones on the front lines witnessing the difficulties their children face from childhood to adulthood.

Mothers often find themselves in the roles of advocate, coach, tutor, social skills facilitator, problem-solver, therapist, scheduler, companion, mediator, disciplinarian, and researcher. We hope they have support from family and friends, but most often, those people don't have a clue what it's like to raise or assist someone with these difficulties. Anyone in this role needs to make self-care a priority since the demands of this "job" can be draining.

Most parents and spouses balk when I suggest they up their self-care game, insisting they don't have the time or the funds. What they don't realize is that eventually the stress will catch up with them. They may experience depression, anxiety, or physical illness. At that point, they may not be able to care for themselves, let alone their child or spouse. My clients who practice self-care are much more resilient and healthier and as a result have better marriages than those who don't practice self-care and nurturing.

I've worked with many parents who have been hurt time and again when looking for support from neurotypical parents' perspectives. NVLD parents must view their role from a different perspective. It's about finding different ways to accomplish goals and holding your child accountable for what they can do and if they can't do something, finding a different way to achieve it. It takes a different mindset, a different way of thinking, which begins in the demystification process. Finding support from others who are in the same boat as you, parenting a neurodivergent, is also a good first step.

A Day in the Life with NVLD

You know my story—now I would like you to meet Lara and James, a mother and son whom I have worked with over the years. Here's Lara's description, in her own words, of what it is like to raise a child with NVLD and her advice from the front lines.

Lara

By the time James was three months old, my husband and I had concerns about his torticollis (twisted neck). At five months, he had low muscle tone and started to miss milestones like crawling and pulling up. We sought an evaluation and were accepted by the Birth to Three Program. By age one, he exhibited stimming—self-stimulating behavior marked by a repetitive action or movement, such as repeatedly tapping on objects or the ears, snapping the fingers, blinking, rocking from side to side, and grunting. Stimming is often associated with autism spectrum disorders, but James did not have that diagnosis. He was given many other diagnoses, though: hypotonia (low muscle tone), poor fine motor skills, poor gross motor skills, sensory integration dysfunction, executive function disorder. A pediatrician at New York University Hospital told us he was a disorganized fourteen-month-old—how right they were! We took him to a developmental psychologist who tested James for autism. He did not score high enough for that diagnosis but came close.

Despite these issues, James was an easy baby and a delightful toddler. He napped, woke up happy, and loved to go on the swings at our local park. People who met him thought that he was so cerebral. He spoke words early, was inquisitive, and had an amazing memory. At one point, he knew the names of all car models!

James was a joy to be with until he got to nursery school, when he began to have trouble mixing with other children and building friendships. Although he had lots of playdates, he was always overwhelmed at some point in the afternoon. He had trouble with tasks like getting snacks because he could not follow multistep directions. So, we knew something was up. His intelligence, however, always shined.

In kindergarten, the school psychologist was concerned about his behavior and suggested he see a neurologist. He received a diagnosis of ADHD.

James's continuous learning and adaptive difficulties at school suggested he might have learning issues. Testing revealed a big discrepancy between his verbal IQ and his performance (nonverbal) IQ. The school psychologist reported James had learning disabilities in addition to ADHD;

dysgraphia, dyscalculia, ADHD, and social skills difficulties were intertwined with overlapping symptoms under the umbrella of NVLD.

NVLD kids love and *need* to sleep! It was hard for James to get up and get going. Getting through his day is exhausting for him. He moves very slowly, so we need to start much earlier to get ready to go anywhere. I gave him verbal reminders as to what he needed to do. Did you brush your teeth, take a shower, *use soap*, put on deodorant? I set out his clothes for the day. Sometimes he did well, and sometimes he had his shirt on backward. But eventually, he got it, and I didn't need to remind him as much.

I often received calls from teachers to tell me that James was having a hard time in the classroom or that he didn't turn in an assignment. One year, I found out in February that he hadn't turned in his homework all year—six months!

At home, he made a mess in the kitchen and living room, leaving cushions, pillows, the remote, and empty glasses everywhere. I helped him pick up and replace the cushions. He still does this. Step by step…

He used to misplace his phone regularly, and we would go over the places he had been in the previous hour or two before. Since the phone is his lifeline, he rarely loses it now.

James tends to stay up late to watch TV or to go on his computer. He doesn't play video games; he *loves* learning. It's amazing to hear what he has gleaned through the internet. He adores audiobooks and podcasts. I'd say that he has taught himself about as much on his own as he has learned from his school.

Yet, self-care, executive functioning, and coordination difficulties are still there. James has a low threshold for daily struggles like rebooting his computer, remembering passwords, and filling out forms. He almost threw a tantrum while we were completing documents for his Social Security disability application.

At nineteen years of age, James has matured a great deal. I do not have to remind him to shower. I do not manage his school schedule. I do not have to remind him to get up for class. He orders his food each day. He seems so motivated with his classes now. We are, however, still working on getting his room tidy.

Many things are difficult for him. Though he often needs assistance, he doesn't always want it. I have found, though, that when he really wants to do something, he is self-motivated and will accomplish tough tasks like showering and dressing or ordering an Uber. Basically, he gets most things, but as he heads toward adulthood, tasks become more complex. I sense that he will keep improving slowly and that he might live with a roommate but need some support until around twenty-five years of age.

James desperately wants acceptance. Although he has a few friends from the private school he attended, he has a hard time figuring out how to be accepted in a new group. He tries hard to fit in, often pretending to be someone he is not and taking on the group's attributes to be included. He is much better on a one-on-one basis. If he is anxious, his social mistakes are exacerbated.

He tends to be too open on social media. He met a thirty-year-old man who offered to help him with his writing. Then the guy became a control freak and started to abuse James. He yelled at James and shamed him. My son wanted this guy to like him so much that we found out he was sending him money to stay on good terms. Eventually, my husband and I had to intervene, and the relationship ended.

With friends, James often comes on too strong, shares too much, and calls or texts too often when the other person is not reciprocating. He desperately needs advice and coaching but doesn't want it from us.

James has endured many instances of bullying. He always loved movies and as he got older, would go to the movies by himself on Friday afternoons. I would give him twenty dollars to grab a Coke at the snack bar. When it was time to pay, James was so nervous that he would say to the cashier, "Is this enough?" and the cashier would say, "Yes." James panicked and did not demand his change, and he would come home empty-handed. This happened for weeks until I spoke to the manager.

Kids at school set him up. They would act like they liked him and then would make fun of him. He was videotaped in the boys' bathroom and verbally abused with words like "retarded." The school administration handled it well, but you can imagine the hit to his self-esteem.

Lots of things at school made him anxious, and talking about it made him feel better. For James, talk therapy was helpful at school and privately. When he needed additional emotional help, we tried a dialectical behavioral therapy (DBT) group. He was not able to process the DBT curriculum, which is built on self-management tasks. The topics go in order, but my son could not suspend whatever was bothering him at the moment to access a particular topic. His DBT therapist offered to meet one on one and insert the curriculum into whatever issue was challenging James. If he was angry, his therapist focused on teaching James relaxation and de-escalation techniques to help him cope. His therapist also took his calls and coached him in real time if he had a problem, such as a disagreement with a friend, or if he had made a social mistake on Facebook. This therapist acted like a life coach, and it worked well.

Lara's Advice for Parents

Get an evaluation as soon as you suspect something is off with your child. When a child is not keeping up academically, parents or the school suggests testing. Don't wait until then. Your state's Birth to Three Program, also known as Early Intervention, is a good place to start. While they cannot give you a concrete diagnosis, they can provide necessary therapy.

If you receive an NVLD diagnosis, read every book on NVLD you can get your hands on. Even better are many Facebook pages devoted to NVLD parents and caregivers and NVLD teens and adults. There you will find that you and your child are not alone. You will receive information, support, suggested therapies, doctors, advice on getting your child into the proper school environment, parenting tips, and success stories. You will be a part of a wonderful community. And you will see how much people with this disorder struggle in many different ways. It will help you to be patient with your own child and with yourself.

While much of their struggles are with life skills, many NVLD individuals shine in academic settings. Let them find their passion, something they are good at, and *indulge* them! My son loves movies and filmmaking. So, he and I attended the film festivals in Toronto, New York, and Tribeca many years in a row. James would research the movies and always found interesting ones to see at these festivals. He would stand up and ask incredibly relevant questions of the actors and directors at the Q&A portion. He was only thirteen or fourteen years old at the time! People around us were amazed, and he was so proud of himself. It did wonders for his self-esteem.

Be a tough advocate for your child during their school years. If your child has an IEP, make sure that it includes accommodations for their anxiety and sensory needs. Homeschooling or small environment schools work well. My son loves to learn. It was the crowded atmosphere and social skills expectations that made school miserable for him. Social skills can be obtained at their own time and pace. Sometimes, surprisingly, social media can actually help them develop communication skills and friendships. Keep a close eye on them with social media, as they are gullible and open to online bullying.

Be prepared to have your heart broken when you see your child hurt by exclusion, bullying, or abuse at school. Some of this will be due to their social mistakes, some not. In their high school years, try to resolve issues with them at home so that you can guide them as to what to do about it. It can make it harder on them if you fight their battles.

Friends come and go. Some NVLDers have a hard time holding on to friendships. Sometimes they come on too strong or incorrectly read social cues. One-on-one friendships are usually easier for them to manage than group dynamics.

Don't rule out college! Your child might not want to go, but don't be surprised if they do. My son wanted to drop out of school after eighth grade. But, during his freshman year of high school, in an after-school film club, he met a couple of high school seniors who were talking about where they were going to college. James came home that night and said, "I want to go to college. What is a GPA?" My husband and I told him we would support him.

It was a tough journey at the time, but he graduated high school and had four college offers—all neurotypical schools, not special education ones. Colleges these days are very accepting of learning differences. James will be getting academic support where he is going and will live at home for at least the first year and maybe the entire time. But he is going to college! There are colleges for everyone, and your son or daughter should go if they want to—even if they don't earn a degree. My son is going to a college where he can choose whatever classes he wants to take—there is no prescribed course plan. And he will take as long as he needs, maybe even five or six years.

I consider most of my parenting a twenty-four-hour therapy session. My NVLD kid needs to talk. He needs to ask questions—that is how he learns about his world. Be prepared to answer and discuss topics over and over. Since some children need to be told explicitly how to do things, there is no way to avoid talking. Learn how to end the conversation when you need a break in a way that doesn't hurt their feelings and provides straightforward feedback to give them help with reading social communication cues. Delivered in a kind and respectful manner, this also gives them the reassurance they need.

Don't let anyone tell you, "You are allowing your son or daughter to be too reliant on you." They need you, and they need you for longer than other children typically need their parents. Don't treat them like a baby, but don't leave them on their own. Stay close but let them try. Keep them accountable and have expectations even if you know that it'll be hard for them to achieve 100 percent of the time. Pick your battles! Let a lot go. Did I say be patient? LOL!

Consider that your child with NVLD might live with you longer than your other children. Plan for it. Also, consider whether they may need Medicaid or Disability for their adult life. Being highly intelligent doesn't mean they don't need support. Make sure you have updated your will with a special needs trust and have your child sign a health-care proxy and power of attorney. There are law firms that will help you draw up those documents. Explain to your child that it is not taking away their rights of decision making.

As far as a career goes, it's so individual. My son will never work a routine job. He will write, podcast, or maybe do stand-up comedy. If he finishes college and gets an advanced degree, he'd like to teach. I have read about the work challenges that exist for NVLD adults on Facebook. I can see that their struggles continue into adulthood, so I am encouraging my son to develop supportive relationships with friends and other organizations, like churches or special interest groups.

My wish for every parent on this journey: patience, love, compassion, humor, self-care, time away, supportive friends and family. Just do the best you can. You got this!

Doing the Best that You Can

Whether you are a parent of a child with NVLD, like Lara, or an adult with NVLD, like me, you cope by doing the best you can. Maya Angelou said, "Do the best you can until you know better. Then when you know better, do better." Doing your best means putting yourself out there and learning from experiences. While you can't completely control the way your brain is wired, you always have the power to do anything to the best of your ability *at that time*. Learn from the experience, tweak your behaviors, and try again. Each time you do this, you are building up your confidence and skill set. Self-compassion and acceptance are the keys to a healthy sense of self.

Let's be real. There are going to be times when doing your best isn't good enough. It's possible that some NVLDers will not be able to button up their shirts, write legibly, process body language efficiently, interpret differences in tone of voice, drive, or cook a tasty meal without ruining it. So what? Yes, it's frustrating, and the outcomes of these difficulties may be less than desirable.

It's OK to do things differently, such as avoiding buttons and zippers by wearing athletic wear, using a voice-to-text writing program, repeating back to others to clarify that you understand the message they intended to communicate, finding a job working from home to reduce the amount of nonverbal communication with others, and buying a frozen lasagna and serving it with a premade salad in a bag. Do what works for you. When you compare yourself to others, you will always come up short until you realize there is no one right way to do anything.

Remember the poem "Autobiography in Five Chapters" at the beginning of this book? You might want to read it now. Chapter III says, "I know where I am. It is my fault [which means it is your choice that got you there]. I get out immediately." Even though we may keep falling into the "hole in the sidewalk," it is our responsibility to get out and then learn how to walk around the hole or down another street.

It is possible to have a better life—it just takes a lot of work. Life is different for each person on the planet, and one's ability to improve it depends on their own skills, available support from others, life circumstances, past experiences, and mental and emotional health. Nonetheless, you and only you can get yourself out of the hole. That requires determination, commitment, and flexibility. Be open to new ideas, try a different approach, and ask for help, and eventually you will succeed.

As a child, a teenager, and a young adult, I struggled with learned helplessness. I tried many things only to fail, over and over. I failed so many times I lost count. I was convinced I would never find anything I could do well. I lost hope. My family and friends told me that "everyone has a talent in something," but that discouraged me even more because I couldn't find one. I retreated into my own world to protect myself from failure.

I suffered bouts of depression so severe that I would spend weeks in bed without bathing and had to force myself to eat. I was so down I couldn't go any lower. The only way I could go was up. I had no choice; I had to figure the way out for myself. It was then I knew this was my purpose in life. I had to go through this suffering so that I could help others.

If you are now where I was then, don't give up! Sure, certain activities may always be challenging for you, but that doesn't determine who you are. And you will never know what you *can* do if you stop trying. Believing in yourself means you need to stop beating your head against the wall about all the things your NVLD has disrupted. Accept yourself, warts and all, and be realistic and persistent. Never give up—that's simply not an option.

What worked for me was proving others wrong. Being told I couldn't do something only fueled my determination. You can do that too. Some roadblocks can be removed, while others need to be navigated. It's up to you which fork in the road you take.

You can either let things happen or make things happen. Making things happen is how I personally achieved success. Being a participant rather than a spectator allows you to create your own opportunities. Work hard and persevere until you find something you can do. The Japanese proverb "Nanakorobi yaoki" means "fall seven times, stand up eight."

A perfect illustration of this proverb is the movie *Rocky*. The scene in the movie where Rocky talks to his son resonated with me and gave me the courage to "keep on keeping."

Rocky says, "Let me tell you something you already know. The world ain't all sunshine and rainbows. It's a very mean and nasty place, and I don't care how tough you are. It will beat you to your knees and keep you there permanently if you let it. You, me, or nobody is gonna hit as hard as life. But it ain't about how hard ya hit. It's about how hard you can get it and keep moving forward. How much you can take and keep moving forward. Now if you know what you're worth, then go out and get what you're worth. But ya gotta be willing to take the hits, not pointing fingers saying you ain't where you wanna be because of him or her or anybody! Until you start believing in yourself you ain't gonna have a life.[3]" I am blessed to have had perseverance. No matter how many times I was knocked down, eventually, I always got back up. Like Rocky says, you too will have to fight for it. As the Japanese say, all you need to do is just keep getting up one more time.

Whenever I felt like giving up, I turned to this movie for encouragement. When you're inspired by a movie or motivational speaker, use your newfound positive energy to fuel your persistence and continue to press forward. The effects of these powerful feelings will only last so long before they begin to fade away. When your enthusiasm is lagging, you can use the lessons and techniques in this book to pump yourself up again.

---

3 (Stallone, Sylvester. 2006. Rocky Balboa. United States: Metro-Goldwyn-Mayer (MGM)

Rocky inspired me: he worked and worked and worked until he got to his goals, and when he did, he set the next bar higher. In my experience, when NDs overcome obstacles, they often find themselves on Cloud 9, so happy they pushed ahead and so proud of their achievements.

I still get back up on my feet each and every time I am knocked down. Like most people, it sometimes takes me a little longer than I'd like, but I get back up and at 'em. What keeps me going? The gratification I feel when I see that my work with others has meant they don't need to suffer like I did

You Too Can Change the World

Steve Jobs's commencement speech to Stanford University students in 2005, in which he quoted Apple's 1997 "Think Different" created by Chiat Day, was a "shout-out" to all those who do think differently:

> Here's to the crazy ones, the misfits, the rebels, the troublemakers, the round pegs in the square holes, the ones who see things differently—they're not fond of rules, and they have no respect for the status quo. You can quote them, disagree with them, glorify or vilify them, but the only thing you can't do is ignore them because they change things. They push the human race forward, and while some may see them as the crazy ones, we see genius, because the people who are crazy enough to think that they can change the world are the ones who do.

I love Steve Jobs. He was quirky and went against the norm when it came to following the traditional route to success. The traditional routes others take don't have to be the same for you. You know yourself better than anyone else, and that, my friend, is going to be the cornerstone of your success. Even though we don't all have the abilities of Steve Jobs, we can learn from him and apply some of his lessons to our lives. You can learn more about him and the three pivotal moments in his life on YouTube.

Acknowledge that it's OK to go your own way, to march to the beat of your own drum. Get in touch with what's in your heart, and follow your instincts. Create your own way, your own path. What makes you tick? What would you do for free and get total enjoyment out of it? What makes you get into your flow? This is what makes you unique, your authentic self.

I took the risk of going from the known to the unknown by leaving my secure teaching career, leaving my tenure, health benefits, and pension behind. To this day, I do not regret it. I was meant to be there for a short time; this job was the catalyst that propelled me to the work I am meant to do: helping others to avoid the pain I experienced by learning from my personal and professional experiences.

That is my destiny, and you have yours. It is just waiting for you to discover it. We all are put here for a reason and have something to contribute to the world, no matter how great or small it is. The only person you should compete against is the you that you were yesterday—every day forward is a win! Don't let the wounds of your past determine who you are and what your future will be.

I hope that my story inspires you to live life with a new perspective on NVLD and the many possibilities that exist for your future. Whether you're a parent of a child or an adult with NVLD, like me and countless others, you can be a success story. Success is defined by many factors, not just how much money you make or the grades your child receives. This book provides the tools you need to begin to put the pieces of the puzzle together to discover and realize your or your child's potential.

It may not be easy, but know you have been heard, acknowledged, and celebrated, like NVLD pioneers David, Kim, Natalie, Bill, Patricia, Sam, Joe, Chloe, and Ted.

Take the rocky road—it's worth it!

Resources for Support and Information

Linda Karanzalis, MS, BCCS
- Author Website: https://www.lindakaranzalis.com
- NVLD Pioneers Free FB Support Group: https://www.facebook.com/NvldPioneers
- Learning Center Website: https://addvantageslearningcenter.com
- Podcast: https://www.lindakaranzalis.com/podcast
- YouTube: https://www.youtube.com/@ADDvantagesLearning

NVLD Project
- https://nvld.org/

Communications
- Active Listening: https://www.bumc.bu.edu/facdev-medicine/files/2016/10/Active-Listening-Handout.pdf
- Bullying: https://www.stopbullying.gov
- "How to Kill Your Body Language Frankenstein (And Inspire the Villagers)," a TEDx Talk delivered by Scott Rouse on YouTube: https://www.youtube.com/watch?v=Ro2dgzXKJfQ

- Reflective Listening: https://www.teaching.unsw.edu.au/group-work-reflective-listening
- Social-Emotional Learning: https://casel.org/

Academics and Career
- Americans with Disabilities Act (ADA): https://www.ada.gov/
- *Employees' Practical Guide to Requesting and Negotiating Reasonable Accommodations Under the Americans with Disabilities Act:* https://askjan.org/publications/individuals/employee-guide.cfm
- Glassdoor: https://www.glassdoor.com
- Information on classroom accommodations: https://www.understood.org/en/articles/at-a-glance-classroom-accommodations-for-nonverbal-learning-disabilities
- Learning Disabilities of America: https://ldaamerica.org/G
- *Mapping Careers with LD and ADD Clients: Guidebook and Case Studies* by Raizy Abby Janus, available from Amazon, Columbia University Bookstore, and Book Depository
- SCORE free advice and support resources for small businesses, available at https://www.score.org.
- State Vocational Rehabilitation Agencies: https://rsa.ed.gov/about/states

Mental Health and Body, Mind, Spirit Modalities

- Advanced Brain Technologies (The Listening Program): https://advancedbrain.com
  Use my code ALC to receive a discount
- Breathing (Wim Hoff free class): https://www.wimhofmethod.com/free-mini-class
- Breathwork and Free Meditations: https://www.ucla-health.org/programs/marc/free-guided-meditations
- Co-Dependents Anonymous: https://coda.org/
- EMDR International Association: https://www.emdria.org
- Emotional Freedom Technique (tapping): https://eftinternational.org
- Energy Psychology: https://www.energypsych.org
- Gratitude: https://www.nami.org/Blogs/NAMI-Blog/September-2016/When-Looking-for-Happiness-Find-Gratitude
- Gut-Brain Connection: https://www.health.harvard.edu/diseases-and-conditions/the-gut-brain-connection
- Identifying Abuse: https://www.thehotline.org/identify-abuse/
- Marc and Angel Hack Life: https://www.marcandangel.com/
- National Association for Holistic Aromatherapy: https://naha.org
- Recovery International: https://www.recoveryinternational.org/

- Reiki: https://reikiassociation.net/home
- RSD (Rejection Sensitive Dysphoria): https://www.webmd.com/add-adhd/rejection-sensitive-dysphoria
- Self-Compassion: https://self-compassion.org/

Author's Note

I wished I had a book like this before I learned about NVLD as the source of all of my struggles. If you feel this book has helped you on your journey with NVLD, please leave a review online of where you purchased it to help spread awareness and hope.

Thank you!

Linda
♥

Printed in Great Britain
by Amazon